DOG TRAINING FOR BEGINNERS

EVERYTHING YOU NEED TO KNOW TO TRAIN
YOUR PET WITH EASY WITH CRATE TRAINING,
POTTY TRAINING, AND OBEDIENCE TRAINING

BRIAN MCMILLAN

PUBLISHING FORTE

INTRODUCTION

If you've picked up this book and decided to glance through the pages, chances are you have some questions about how to train your dog. Welcome to the club—you're in good company!

The truth is that almost every dog owner will encounter a behavioral or training issue at some point in their dog's life. This is entirely normal. Dogs are amazing creatures, but they don't come preprogrammed with an understanding of human rules and expectations—and they don't speak English, so teaching them what we want can be challenging.

Figuring out how to wrangle your wild-eyed, barking, leash-pulling furry friend into a polite and well-mannered companion can seem like a daunting task at first. Fortunately, the solutions are often simpler than you might think; you just need a clear training plan and a little motivation.

I've worked with thousands of dogs over the last 15 years and dedicated myself to helping people and dogs live better together. That's my mission statement and what I want this book to do for you: to make your life with your dog more enjoyable every day.

The following pages will provide simple, actionable training solutions for common problems. Really—that's it! No long, technical dissertations on the intricate minutiae of learning theory or complicated twelve-week programs designed to transform your life and that of your pet. These things have their place, but I want this book to be something different.

And this "something different" is easy to read and addresses your needs without wasting your time.

As you will see, each of the following sections is devoted to an area of concern that might interest you, ranging from a quick crash course on dog training in general to specific advice on common training issues and basic obedience, handling and grooming, tricks and games, and even higher-level behavioral concerns such as aggression and anxiety.

It takes work, but it's not that hard once you know what to do. I'll break everything down, so you know exactly what to do to keep moving you and your dog forward in the right direction. As you move along, remember that it's about progress, not perfection. Every dog is different: some will understand things very easily, while other dogs may require a little more work. And you undoubtedly have other responsibilities and stuff going on in your life—most people can't just drop every-thing to train a dog full time—so give yourself a break and don't put too much pressure on yourself. Together, we'll create an environment where you and your dog know exactly what you need to do to make each other happy.

Whatever your specific problem might be, I hope you'll find this book helpful!

1

DOG TRAINING BASICS

Dogs are so integrated into our human society that we often forget that they are quite different from us, think a little differently, and have different needs. That being said, their behavior patterns, motivations, and desires can be very similar to ours. Once you understand the basic principles of dog training, you'll be able to see how everything fits together. In the beginning, you may want to refer back to this chapter every now and then to reinforce the basics of training your dog and keep the fundamentals in mind.

The Most Important Things To Remember About Dog Training

On the following few pages are the nine things I believe are most important when training your dog. You should always keep them in mind and use them in your daily interactions, communication, and training with your dog. There's plenty more I could add to this list, but these are the big ones that are critical to getting the results you want.

Positive Reinforcement

Training dogs (and other animals) using positive reinforcement is very effective. Positive reinforcement is doing something immediately after a behavior occurs to increase the frequency of that behavior.

THE PHRASE IS TECHNICALLY BROKEN down into two pieces. Reinforcement occurs when a behavior is repeated or increased in frequency (it is not reinforcement if the behavior decreases).

POSITIVE IMPLIES that something has been added. For instance, you instruct the dog to sit, he sits, and reward him with a treat (something is added). When you ask the dog to sit again, he is more likely to do so (the behavior was reinforced).

Repetition

All behavior, including yours, is created by repeating something over time until it becomes a habit. Your dog will tend to do whatever he's repeatedly done, especially if it's rewarding. But the longer a negative behavior has been going on, the more repetitions it will take to reshape it. To get a great dog, you must get your dog to do the good behaviors more often while limiting the number of mistakes he makes. Dog training is really just steering your dog to do all the behaviors you like more often. Once enough repetitions of good behavior have been made (the exact number will differ for every dog), your dog will continue them out of habit.

· · ·

IF YOU'RE NOT CAREFUL, though, repetitions can really hurt you. If your dog is having trouble with a particular skill that you're trying to teach him, it just means you haven't done enough repetitions to make the behavior stick yet. Take a small step back in the training process and do some more repetitions. Every dog will progress at their own pace; some dogs may need more repetitions or work on a specific skill than others.

Consistency

Your dog will learn much faster if everyone in the family is on the same page, has the same rules, and is teaching her the same things. If you've been diligent about not letting your dog on the sofa, but your daughter has been letting her come up, your dog is getting mixed signals and will never understand what you expect of her. I recommend you have a family meeting to go over the rules for your dog, including what's allowed, what's not allowed, and how you train her. Make sure everyone understands them and is in agreement.

IF YOU ALL stay consistent in what you want and how you communicate with your dog, there won't be any confusion, and you'll see much more progress than if everyone is doing their own thing. The best way to speed up your results is to increase the repetitions of the behavior while maintaining strong consistency throughout the training process.

Perseverance

There's one big roadblock you'll encounter as you begin working with your dog, and how you handle it will decide whether you succeed or struggle. We live in a world of immediate gratification and expect to get what we want fast—like right now! This isn't a problem for things like Internet speed or lunch orders. With dog training, however, this expectation creates unrealistic expectations that lead to frustration and disappointment.

YOU HAVE to understand that training your dog takes time. You will need to get the repetitions in and allow your dog to go through the learning process. Some dogs will need more work to get certain skills, but if you stick with them, any dog is capable of learning. If you're not seeing the compliance you want, it just means that you haven't done enough repetitions to effectively shape the behavior yet. Keep going!

PATIENCE IS NOT one of my strong points, so I know this can be challenging. Just know that every dog starts not knowing what you want them to do, but if you can keep practicing with your dog, you'll be amazed at what he can learn.

Timing

You've probably heard the phrase "timing is everything." Well, that's never been more relevant than with training a dog. When you ask your dog to do something, delivering the reward to her is critical to helping your dog understand what you want her to do. If your timing is spot-on, she'll learn more quickly, and training will be easy. However, if your timing is off, it can confuse your dog and leave you both frustrated.

.   .   .

DOGS ARE VERY PRESENT-MINDED ANIMALS, meaning they live in the here and now. You have a two- to three-second window to reward your dog after he does something you like for him to connect the behavior with the reward. This way, he will realize that you like what he just did and that he should do it more often to get more of the stuff he loves. For example, let's say you're working on teaching your dog to come when called in the backyard. You call him over, and he runs to you like a good dog. You realize you don't have any treats at that moment, so you go inside your house with your dog following you, walk to your kitchen, enter the treat jar, and give your dog his reward. Congrats—you just rewarded your dog for standing in your kitchen. The recall you did outside was 12 long seconds ago, and your dog will never make that connection.

SO BE PREPARED when working with your dog on a desired behavior. Have your treats on hand for immediate rewards for good repetitions, so she knows exactly what you liked and want more of. This is especially critical when you're just starting out and can really speed up your dog's learning.

Communication

One of the big problems between dogs and humans is that we speak two very different languages. We default to verbal communication, while our dogs prefer nonverbal (yes, even those barky pups). Very early on, our dogs realize that we talk and talk and talk and very little of the talk has anything to do with them. So, our dogs begin to ignore our speech. They just hear, "Blah, blah, blah, blah, treat, blah, blah, blah, walk, blah, blah . . ." They've learned to tune us out because most of what we say isn't for them. Just think how much you talk around your dog throughout an average day: on the phone, with the kids, to the TV during your favorite sporting event. It goes on all day long and teaches our dogs not to pay attention to what we say. To combat this, you must talk less when communicating with your dog. Keep it short and sweet; the fewer words the better. If you're asking your dog to sit, simply say "Sit." Not "Okay, honey, can you please sit for me?" Avoid using sentences. Just keep it simple and to the point.

HOW YOU SAY THINGS MATTERS, too. Dogs respond to confidence, so make sure you say things like you believe they will happen. If you don't believe it, your dog won't either and will be less likely to listen to you. You don't want to be too forceful about it, just say it like you're sure of yourself.

Focus

Once you get going and see how well your dog responds and how much you both are enjoying the training process, you may want to do more of it right away. Your dog might be doing so great at "sit" that you want to add in "down" and "come," as well. There are so many useful and fun things you can teach your dog, but make sure you're not doing too much at one time. If you're training a bunch of new skills simultaneously, you risk diluting the results and making it hard for your dog to master any skill.

INSTEAD, it's best to only focus on teaching one new thing at a time and practice it until you get 90 percent compliance. Only then should you add in something else. Try not to put too much pressure on your dog to learn too many things simultaneously. Give him enough time to get good at one thing so he can remember it long-term. Once he's got a solid foundation with a skill, you can layer in another and continue building his knowledge base.

Motivation

I always like to think about the dog's perspective and try to understand what's going through his mind as he lives with us funny humans. The main thing to remember about all dog training is that you never want to force your dog to do anything. That's very limiting and doesn't work all that well over the long term. Instead, you want him to want to do all the behaviors that you prefer. To accomplish this, you just need to show your dog that it's in his best interest to do things your way. Remember that your dog always thinks, "What's in it for me?" Your dog will happily repeat good behavior if you can figure out what he wants and give it to him only after he has done something well.

REMEMBER that every dog will value different things, so you don't always have to use food and treats to reward your dog. The cool thing about dogs is that they love the simple pleasures in life. Going for a walk, affection, and play are all great life rewards for your dog. For some dogs, a game of tug is better than any treat. Experiment and see what your dog likes and responds to the best, then use all his favorite rewards throughout the day as you work with him.

Flexibility

Training your dog is really about building a relationship. You're spending time learning to communicate and understand each other while creating the structure of how you relate to each other. The relationship between a person and their dog is much like that between a parent and child.

THE PARENT SETS RULES, boundaries, and consequences to create a well-mannered adult. That's exactly what you're doing with your furry child, too. Once you've put in the time and built the relationship, your dog will be more likely to listen to you in other situations and environments. The only problem is that you can't transfer your relationship to someone else—they have to do the work and build their relationship with the dog.

IT'S like when a new babysitter comes along, and the kids won't listen. Who do you think the kids would listen to? The old babysitter, of course, because they had built a relationship, but the new babysitter hasn't yet. So, if everyone in the family wants the dog to listen to them, everyone needs to spend time building a relationship.

YOU ALSO WANT to vary the places and situations where you do things with your dog. If you only practice sit in the living room, you might not get that behavior in the kitchen. Make sure you practice skills in different places, under different conditions, and with different distractions. The more you mix up where and how you do the training, the more compliance you'll see from your dog.

This Is Your Dog's Brain

Ever wonder what your dog is thinking? Of course, you have —we all want to know what's going on in that cute little furry head. I believe dogs are not all that different from you and me. They want to live a good life, which includes doing more of the stuff they like and less of the stuff they don't like. A dog's quest is to figure out how to get all the good things in life and keep them coming as much as possible. Yeah, I can relate.

DOGS ARE ALSO emotional animals that crave social interaction and form strong bonds. Seeing the look in my dog's eyes when I come home, combined with the wiggle in his little butt, makes me doubtless that he loves me more than most of my human relatives. Through domestication, dogs have become very attached to us. They like our company, are eager to please us, and get just as much out of our companionship as we do theirs.

DOGS FEEL VARIOUS EMOTIONS, including fear, love, disgust, and excitement, just like humans do. And just as we can make bad decisions when we're emotional, so can our dogs. That's why it's so important to cultivate a calm, peaceful mind by not rewarding any of their negative emotional states of mind. Excitement is the negative emotional state of mind I see the most with my clients. So often, people either intentionally or inadvertently reward excitement, which causes the dog to make poor decisions. I don't treat jumping because a calm dog doesn't jump. Consider your dog's state of mind when giving any reward. And remember, rewards are more than just treats and food—there are also life rewards.

YOU GET WHAT YOU REWARD. If you reward a happy dog, you'll get a happy dog more often, especially in the situation where you gave the reward. The same holds true of negative emotions. You'll get a more anxious dog if you reward an anxious one. Take thunderstorms, for example—many dogs develop anxiety around storms. Thunder booms overhead, and your dog gets startled, understandably, and shows signs of anxiety—tail tucked under his body, ears back, maybe shaking a little. You will probably see that and want to make him feel better, so you'll gently pet him and tell him in a soothing voice that everything will be okay.

THE PROBLEM IS that your dog can't understand your words; he just makes associations. In that scenario, your dog will pair the stimulus (the thunder) with his state of mind (anxious) when he received the reward (petting and affection). Then, the next time the trigger of thunder happens, he'll go back to the anxiety associated with it. You don't want to reward anything you don't like. What you can do in that situation is not give it much attention. Pretend it's no big deal, ignore the anxiety, and see if you can give your dog another experience. Try to catch him before the "scary" stimulus and do something fun like play so that he's focused on something positive when the thunder comes. Or, if he's already showing signs of being scared, try to snap him out of it with a fun game or simple task, then reward that. This can give him a new, positive experience with the encounter.

2

TRAINING EQUIPMENT AND SUPPLIES YOU WILL NEED

I'll start off with the supplies you'll need for basic training and everyday use. These are items that just about everyone will need, especially in the beginning, and will make up the core of your toolbox. Because you will use these every day, make sure that both you and your dog like them and are comfortable with them.

SOME ITEMS LIKE A CRATE, leash, or collar can be purchased and used if they are in good condition, but inspect them thoroughly and wash everything before using them for your dog.

Crate

A crate is a must for dogs, but I also recommend one for any new dog coming into your home, regardless of its age.

. . .

FIRST OFF, let me assure you that putting your dog in a crate is not a negative thing—at least not if you do it right. If done properly, your dog should love her crate.

DOGS ARE natural den animals that have the innate desire to keep their den clean and not pee or poop in it. This makes the crate the best tool for house-training. Your dog can also get into a lot of trouble running around your house, so you need a safe place to put her when you can't supervise. The crate will become the safe spot where you can leave her and go take a quick shower or run some errands without worrying whether she's doing some bad repetitions of eating your sofa.

THE SIZE of the crate will depend on the size of your dog. For house-training purposes, the crate should be nice and snug, just roomy enough for her to stand and turn around but not large enough that she can comfortably pee in one corner and sleep in the other. If you have a puppy, I recommend getting a generic wire crate that comes with a divider so you can start small and expand it as she grows.

YOU CAN PUT a blanket or bed in the crate to start off. However, if your dog pees on it or chews it up, remove it and leave the crate bare at first. Some dogs will shred any bedding you put in there when they are bored. Plush, rope, and squeaky toys are usually only fun when you're on the other end of them, so I recommend not leaving them in the crate. It's also possible that your dog may chew off pieces and swallow them. You can set aside some sturdier chew toys to give your dog something fun to do while she's spending some time alone. You don't want your dog to get into the habit of going to bed when you do, so don't leave anything in the crate overnight.

ONCE YOUR DOG learns the rules, is totally house-trained, and can be trusted not to get into mischief, it's your choice if you want to keep the crate or get rid of it. My little guy still loves his crate.

Collar and Harness

It's a good idea to always keep a collar on your dog that contains your contact information (either on a tag or sewn into the collar) just in case she ever wanders off. There are a ton of different collars out there with all kinds of gizmos to fasten them to your dog. However, I prefer the old-fashioned buckle collar over anything else. I've tried the adjustable collars with the quick-release plastic closure, but they loosen up over time. A nylon collar with a metal buckle will never loosen up and, if fitted properly, will stay on your dog's neck no matter what.

I ALSO RECOMMEND you get your dog microchipped. If your dog ever gets lost and doesn't have her collar on, the microchip is the only way someone will be able to identify you as her owner and return her to you. Just ask your vet to check if your dog has already been microchipped and, if not, it's super easy to get it done. If you're adopting a rescue dog that already has a microchip, make sure to update the chip records with your name and address.

. . .

Breed Considerations

Sighthounds like greyhounds, Italian greyhounds, and whippets have heads that are the same size as their necks, which causes most collars to slip right over their heads. If you have one of these breeds, you should only use a martingale collar, which consists of two loops (one big, one small) that when pulled tight make it impossible to back out of.

A harness that attaches the leash on the dog's back is a better choice for some dogs who have physical limitations, like dachshunds, pugs, and English bulldogs as well as some small breed dogs. Back-attaching harnesses can also be used on other dogs, but strong dogs or ones that pull on the leash can be a challenge to handle. For those dogs, I recommend a front-attaching harness that will make it easier to accomplish loose leash walking.

Leashes

There is a wide variety of leashes that serve many different purposes. For most walks and training, you'll need a simple six-foot-long leash. This length keeps your dog fairly close, yet still gives her some room to sniff and check things out. The thickness of the leash will depend on the size of your dog and your personal preference. I feel more comfortable with a thicker, rounded leash as opposed to a thin or flat one. If you don't have a secure, fenced-in area, you might also want to get a long line (30 to 50 feet) to use when teaching your dog to come.

· · ·

THE ONE TYPE of leash I really don't like is the retractable leash. These give you very little control and make it harder to communicate with your dog. At worst, they can harm both you and your dog. They may have their place in a big open field but not in a typical residential area. First off, a walk is a team activity, and if your dog is 10 to 26 feet in front of you, you're not even on the same walk. You want your dog somewhat close so you can influence his decision-making and have control if you need it. If your dog darts after a squirrel, you're going to have a very hard time reeling her in. She may even take you off your feet or run into the street. I've also seen people get some really bad injuries when the cord of a retractable leash gets wrapped around them.

Training Treats

You can experiment with lots of different kinds and flavors of treats for snacks or special rewards, but for training purposes, I recommend using something small, about the size of a pea, because you may be giving a lot of them in a training session.

SOMETHING MEAT-BASED with a lot of scent is more motivating for your dog. Nothing does the job like freeze-dried liver, which can be stored at room temperature and comes in small bite-sized pieces that are great for a medium or large dog. You will need to break them up if you've got a little pooch. They're great for training rewards, and because they have a strong smell that is appealing to dogs, they're a great choice when working around distractions.

Additional Dog Supplies

Now let's look at some things that will help you take care of your dog. These are items that just about everyone with a dog will need and use regularly throughout the life of their furry best friend. A lot of this stuff is subjective, so you'll have to test out different varieties to see which ones you and your dog like best. Let's take a look at some of my favorite general dog supplies.

Food

It can be challenging to find the right food and diet for you and your dog among the wide variety of options available. There's dry food, canned wet food, and home-prepared and raw food diets. Nutrition is a very personal thing, and not everyone agrees on the best kind of diet to feed a dog. So instead of telling you which food to give your dog, I'm going to give you some basic guidelines. Then, I recommend you do some additional research to figure out what you'll feed your dog. Always read the labels and look for short ingredients lists with natural foods you recognize, like salmon and barley. Try to avoid dog foods with lots of preservatives, artificial colors, and fillers.

BE careful when you're switching your dog's diet, too. Even though you may be transitioning to a higher-quality food, the change may still cause some stomach upset as your dog adjusts. Don't switch to a different food all at once. Instead, gradually add in the new food to the existing diet and slowly adjust the ratio over two to three weeks.

Food and Water Dishes

Your dog will need separate bowls for food and water. Stainless steel bowls are a must for water, but I also recommend them for food. Plastic bowls harbor bacteria in the cuts and crevasses they get, and many ceramic bowls are made with harmful glazes. Stainless steel bowls are a very safe choice that will last a lifetime. They are also dishwasher safe, rustproof, and pretty much indestructible. I recommend washing them often to keep them clean and sanitary. If you're feeding a raw diet, you should always wash the bowl after each feeding.

THERE'S a bit of controversy over whether raised feeders are good or bad for large breed dogs, but it seems that the current consensus is that they may contribute to bloat, so it's best to avoid them.

FRESH WATER SHOULD BE MADE available to your dog at all times with the exception of house-training puppies, in which case you may want to limit water consumption to specific times of day.

Bones

Bones can be a great way to keep your dog happily occupied as well as keep her teeth clean. Much like with food, look for natural bones that are not processed and do not have artificial additives. There are many healthy options like bully sticks and tendons, but avoid rawhide bones. Rawhide is not completely digestible and can cause a blockage in a dog's intestine. Also, never give your dog any cooked bones because they can splinter and create sharp edges that can be life-threatening once ingested. Always supervise your dog when she's chewing on a bone and take it away if it gets too small so she doesn't try to swallow a big chunk of it.

DEER ANTLERS, which you can find in most pet stores and online, are also good for dogs that like to chew. They are slightly more expensive but will last for years, if not forever.

Chew Toys

There are also a bunch of cool toys designed to give your pooch a good outlet for chewing so he will stay clear of your furniture. These toys are typically made of pressed nylon or a similar material and can be pretty durable, even for aggressive chewers. They usually have added flavor as extra motivation for your dog and are available in a number of different sizes. It's good to have at least one of these accessible to your dog so he always has good activity choices.

General Dog Toys

Most dogs, especially young ones, are goofballs that love to play. Getting your dog some toys to play with will help her burn off some energy. They are also a great way to have fun and bond with her. Every dog has its own personal favorites, so you may have to experiment with a few different kinds to figure out what your pooch likes. There's everything from rope and squeaky toys to plush and crinkly toys to balls of all kinds. Bring a few different options home and see which ones your dog enjoys playing with the most.

. . .

JUST BE careful with any small pieces that your dog might be tempted to chew off and swallow. As with bones, it's best to supervise her while she's playing and take the toy away if she's able to break off pieces or it begins to fall apart. My little guy is an obsessive chewer and can't be trusted with any toy. He will methodically chew it apart and eat it piece by piece. His motto is "Swallow it first, then decide if it was edible." (I learned that the hard way.)

Interactive Toys

Playing with toys with your dog is lots of fun, but sometimes you have human stuff that needs to get done and you don't have the time to play. The problem with most dog toys is that they're only really fun for your dog if you're there throwing the ball, tugging the rope, or engaging her with it. Interactive toys fill that gap and incentivize your dog to play by herself.

THESE TOYS HOLD food or treats inside of them to motivate your pup to keep playing until she's able to get the goodies. My all-time favorite is the Kong, which you can find in almost any pet store. A Kong looks like a rubber hollowed-out snowman. The toy by itself is not that impressive, but when you fill it with yummy stuff, it can keep your dog busy for a while. I recommend putting something semi-moist inside and then freezing it so that it takes your dog longer to get the food out. Peanut butter, canned pumpkin, plain yogurt, and wet dog food work great. If you don't put it in the freezer, most dogs will only take about five minutes to get it all out, but a frozen Kong should buy you about 15 to 20 minutes. You can also try out different puzzle games and toys that use food to see what your dog likes and what keeps her interested.

Dog Bed

Whether you use a crate for your dog, give her free rein of the house, or let her sleep in bed with you, she still needs a comfy place that is all her own. I like to have at least one dog bed available so my dog knows he always has a bed to snooze in any time, regardless of who's home and using up the other comfortable areas. I keep at least one bed on every floor of my house because my pooch tends to wander where we humans do. Even though we allow him on the furniture and in our beds, he often chooses his own beds over these seemingly more desirable places.

MUCH LIKE ALL other dog products, there's an array of dog beds to choose from. Observe the kinds of places your dog prefers to sleep and use that as a guide to pick a bed that's she'll be happy with. I noticed my dog likes to curl up in a tight ball and press his face against something, so I got him a tight round bed with plush walls, which he took to immediately. Make sure the bed is easily washable, and throw it in the washing machine about once a month to keep it clean. It's also best to use unscented detergent so you don't overwhelm your dog's nose with fragrances.

Poop Bags

All right, let's talk poop— maybe not poop specifically, but poop cleanup. It's not the glamorous side of sharing your life with a dog, but it's one of the (smelly) realities, and one that you're going to need to take care of. Cleaning up after your dog is not optional; it's mandatory. If everyone just left their dog's poop where they did their business, the world would be a pretty stinky and disgusting place. Take pride in your community, be a good neighbor, and always pick up your dog's poop.

IT'S NOT HARD, and with all the bags on the market today, it's easy to get some poop bags with a convenient holder that can be fastened right to your leash so you're ready anytime your dog feels nature calling. You can even buy bags that are scented so the rest of your walk doesn't stink, and many of them are biodegradable.

NOTE: I typically don't recommend any of the products designed for indoor cleanup of accidents, such as enzyme sprays. They are typically just regular cleaners with a label to target pet owners. In the small amount that you'll use, the ingredients in regular cleaning products are not a danger and I've never heard of anyone ever having a bad experience with them. There is also very little that will deter your dog from going on the same spot again. Those products are more about good marketing than usefulness, in my opinion.

3

DOG PROOFING - PREPARING YOUR HOME

J ust a quick reminder: When you get a dog, you're inviting another species into your home. Your dog has no idea how to live in your very human world. The cool thing is that dogs are very adaptable and trainable if you take the time to teach them what they need to do (and not do). By default, dogs will act like, well, dogs. This can include peeing on your expensive carpet, lying all over your comfy couch, and maybe even taking a few bites out of your designer shoes. To ensure none of that happens, you must prepare your home to set your new furry friend up to succeed.

Clear the Way

Before you "release the hounds!" in your house, you need to make sure you do a little dog-proofing. It's not just for young pups, either. Remove all objects that will likely tempt your new dog. I recommend looking at your living spaces through the eyes of a dog. Yep, that means getting on your hands and knees and eyeballing everything from a dog's perspective.

Look at lower shelves to see if any objects would be accessible to him and be aware of spaces he might get into. Things look very different from our perspective, so if you don't get down to your dog's eye level, you might miss some stuff that could be potentially dangerous to him. Plus, you will save your valuables from teeth marks and destruction.

KEEP in mind that removing everything is a smart way to start, but if you want your dog to live in a world that includes shoes, plants, and that ugly rug your mother-in-law got you, you'll need to work with your dog around those items when you can supervise him closely. In the beginning, it's best to start with as few distractions as you can manage. Slowly bring your household items back into a controlled setting once you've had some time to build your relationship and get your dog acclimated to his new home.

Remove Choking Hazards

Dogs are like babies when it comes to exploring their world —everything will go into their mouths. This is further amplified in dogs because they don't have hands, so they lead with their mouth. This is normal and to be expected, but it can be dangerous. You must remove anything small enough for your dog to swallow. That also includes anything that they could feasibly bite into pieces. There's nothing worse than an expensive and scary visit to the veterinarian to get an object removed from inside your dog's stomach.

AS A GENERAL RULE, assume your dog will try to eat it, whatever it is. This is definitely a better-safe-than-sorry approach, so don't gloss over it. Make sure you do an initial sweep of your house, then regularly look it over to ensure nothing is missed. Check small spaces, like the gap between your bed and your nightstand—curious puppies and small dogs can often squeeze into areas that seem too tiny to accommodate a dog. As your dog learns how to live among all this interesting human stuff without sampling it, he will build the habit of leaving it alone, and you can relax and be less vigilant.

Relocate or Store Your Valuables

In addition to assessing and removing all of the small objects around your home, it's also a good idea to temporarily remove some of your furniture and any sentimental and expensive items you want to protect. I don't mean to give you the impression that your new dog will come into your house like a wrecking ball, laying waste to everything in his path. Every dog is so different, and some will be well-mannered and respectful of all your stuff right out of the gate. But others can be destructive, and I just want to ensure you're prepared for whatever may happen. I wouldn't want you to start your relationship with your new dog feeling angry and resentful of him because he made some early mistakes at the expense of your new living room furniture.

So, look around your house for anything you would really be upset over if it was damaged. Those items should be removed temporarily until your dog has acclimated and you feel you can trust him. Area rugs you like should be rolled up and put in storage, favorite chairs moved to other rooms of the house that will be off-limits to your dog, and any antiques or furniture with sentimental value put out of sight. This is especially important with puppies since they are pretty much guaranteed to have accidents on the floor and will try to chew on everything.

Ditch the Dangers

In addition to removing everything you value, you also need to make sure there is nothing accessible that could be harmful to your dog if he were to get ahold of it. Believe it or not, many common items you love and use without any problems can harm your dog. It's important to know exactly what these items are and make sure you rearrange your environment so your dog can't get to them. You may have to dispose of some things entirely because the risk is just not worth it. Safety first!

POISONS: Several items toxic to dogs can be found in every home, so it's important to note these and ensure your dog stays away from them.

PHARMACEUTICALS: Both prescription and over-the-counter medication can harm your dog and should always be kept out of reach. Even drugs that are prescribed for your dog by the veterinarian can be dangerous if he consumes a large quantity.

HOUSE PLANTS: Many plants and flowers that you find in and around your house are not safe for dogs. The most common are tulips, sago palm, oleander, philodendrons, rhododendron (also known as azaleas), mistletoe, autumn crocus, and English ivy.

. . .

ESSENTIAL OILS: Essential oils can sometimes be used to help humans and dogs with several different ailments. However, others can be harmful if used on or consumed by your dog. Don't assume that just because it's good for you, it will have the same effect on your dog. Consult your veterinarian before using any essential oil for your dog.

CLEANING SUPPLIES: Just about anything you use to clean is not good for your dog to ingest, so keep all supplies securely stored.

PESTICIDES: If you're treating your lawn or house with any chemical insecticide or fertilizer, check to ensure it's pet-safe. If you use a landscaper, check with them about what they use on your lawn.

People Food

Although your dog can get along just fine eating a commercial dog food exclusively, supplementing his diet with whole foods or just surprising him with a special treat now and then is a sure fire way to put a smile on his face. One thing to remember is that you want to ensure you're rewarding him for good behavior (not begging at the table) and never go from your plate to his bowl. You don't want him to equate your food with his food. Some foods like apples, carrots, bananas, blueberries, and just about any meat (the less seasoned, the better) are great for dogs, but some foods are harmful and even potentially life-threatening.

. . .

CHOCOLATE: Chocolate contains theobromine and caffeine and is a big no-no for dogs. I know of a few dogs that died after eating it, so be very careful. The most dangerous kinds are baking chocolate and dark chocolate.

ONIONS AND GARLIC: These can damage red blood cells and make a dog anemic.

GRAPES AND RAISINS: These are very toxic to dogs and can cause kidney failure.

APPLE SEEDS: Apples are good, but the seeds should be removed. If your dog chews them, they can release cyanide (from the natural chemical amygdalin found in apples) when digested.

AVOCADOS: These contain persin, which can cause vomiting, diarrhea, and heart congestion. That big pit is also a choking hazard.

COFFEE AND TEA: These can cause vomiting, elevated heart rate and blood pressure, seizures, and even death.

MACADAMIA NUTS: These are very dangerous for dogs and can cause muscle shakes, vomiting, a rise in temperature, and weakness in the back legs.

Don't Be Shocked

No matter where you live or what kind of a lifestyle you have, we are part of a very plugged-in society. It's great for enjoying the modern conveniences of life, but it poses some potential problems for our dogs. As I mentioned, dogs like to explore their world with their mouths. To your dog, electrical cords look tasty, feel like a nice chew, and seem like a logical thing to play with, so you need to be very careful.

CHEWING up the cords of your electronics will not only get you all steamed up, but it can also be hazardous if your dog ingests them. A cord may also deliver a jolt of electricity. Supervision is critical to ensuring your dog is not tempted by all those cords and teaching him that they are not there for his enjoyment. Remember, keep your eyes on your dog at all times in the beginning as you learn what kinds of things attract his attention.

Limit Access to Other Rooms

There's a good chance that everything your new dog sees in your house is brand-new and exciting to him. If you've adopted an older dog, you really don't know what he's experienced in his life so far, and if you have a puppy, it's definitely all new to him. When presented with novel stuff, dogs will want to explore, investigate, and sample, which might not be the best thing for you or him. Your job is to supervise him along the way and teach him what things he can interact with and which items in your home are off-limits to him.

· · ·

THE BEST WAY TO accomplish this is to keep his world small and then slowly expand it as he learns. If you give him too much freedom too quickly, you'll set him up to make mistakes. Start small by only giving him access to a few rooms and then letting him acclimate. You can expand his environment to include more rooms when he's doing well. Supervise closely to see how he handles the new areas whenever you give him more freedom. Keep expanding his world as he shows he's ready—his behavior will dictate how fast you can open things up for him. Depending on how your house is laid out, you can use baby gates and closed doors to remove access to certain rooms. Keep in mind that larger and smaller athletic dogs may figure out they can jump right over the gates if they are motivated enough.

Accidents Will Happen

Even if you've adopted an adult dog described as fully house-trained, you should expect a few accidents as she gets acclimated. Coming into a new home can be stressful, and although your dog may have had a good habit of only going outside before, she doesn't have any history in your house and may get a little confused at first. This is perfectly normal and nothing to worry about. In the beginning, ensure you're taking her out often—even more often than she should be capable of holding it—to give her many chances to get it right. This is how to start building the repetitions that will shape her habit of only going to the bathroom outside her new house.

REMOVING any area rugs or other furniture you care about for the first month or two is a good idea. Once your dog has been doing well and you're confident that she's developed the habit of going outside, you can bring all your furniture back again.

Securing the Yard

Having a nice fenced-in yard for your dog to play in is great, but always remember the golden rule: Dogs will act like dogs. I see too many people open their back door and let Fido out to get some exercise while they go back inside. News flash: Your dog won't just endlessly run laps by himself. He will find something to do, which may include digging holes in the center of the Earth, eating your flowers, and barking at the neighbors—all of which are repetitions and habits you don't want. So, like with everything else, your dog needs your guidance to teach him how to behave. It would be best if you were outside to reward him for doing the right things and to correct the behaviors you don't like.

BEFORE YOU GET THERE, it's a good idea to take a walk through your yard and scan for anything that might not be safe for your dog. Walk the entire fence line looking for gaps at the bottom or holes in the sides that your dog could escape through, including those that you think are too small to be of concern—some dogs are born escape artists! Then look at the objects you have in your yard. Is there anything that he can swallow or chew up? If so, remove them for now. Once your dog is doing well, you can reintroduce them and see how he does. Finally, check to see what trees, bushes, and plants you have growing back there and ensure none of them are toxic to dogs.

Rally the Troops

As I mentioned in chapter one, it's a good idea to start by having a family meeting to discuss what bringing a dog into your home really means, how life will change, and what rules you will have. Ensure everyone is on the same page. If your whole family understands the rules and is united on the training procedures, your new dog will fit in much better. Go over how you will limit your dog's boundaries and ensure everyone in your family understands their role.

LET every family member know that, for dogs, "love" is spelled T-I-M-E. If they want to have a strong relationship with your new pup, they need to spend time with him. Whoever spends the most time with your dog (especially doing the things he loves most, like feeding, walking, and playing) will probably get the most attention from him.

Care Tip: Dog Rules for Kids

1. Don't wrestle or play with your dog with your hands. Always play with a toy.
2. Don't hug your dog (because he really doesn't like that).
3. Don't put your face right into his.
4. Speak calmly to him. No yelling.
5. Make him do something good before giving him a treat. A simple "sit" is great.
6. Don't pet or bother him while he's chewing on a bone. Please give him a little space to enjoy it.
7. Be careful when opening the front door so your dog doesn't try to sneak outside.

8. Clean up all your toys. If your stuff is on the floor, your dog might chew it up.

9. Always wash your hands after feeding, walking, or playing with your dog.

10. If your dog is sleeping, don't surprise him. Instead, let him know you're there and see if he wants to come over to you. If not, respect that he's tired and let him rest.

4

WELCOMING YOUR NEW BEST FRIEND

A s your life with your new dog begins, and you start to get to know each other, keep one thing in mind: It's all about the relationship. How your dog responds and acts around you directly reflects the kind of relationship you've created. Notice my words there. Your relationship isn't something you get; it's something you create. It's up to you to set the tone and build the foundation for a strong, healthy relationship with your new dog.

You'll hear many people say you need to be "the leader" and you have to "show them who's boss." Although I agree that dogs need a stable leader and be shown what to do, I don't like the tone that those phrases project. It's not about being militant or bossy. It should be done benevolently. Don't think of it as being a boss; think of it as being a parent. Your relationship with your dog is very similar to that of a parent and child. There are rules, boundaries, and consequences that are set and enforced by the parent. Kids and dogs both thrive with structure, and you, the parent, are the one who needs to create that. This chapter will cover some ways you can provide that structure and help your dog adjust to her new home with you.

Bring Spot Home

The day is finally here! Your new furry best friend is coming home to join your family. This is a very exciting time for both you and your new dog. You've been anticipating and planning for this moment and prepared everything for their arrival. Your new dog, however, is not quite as prepared. She doesn't understand what's happening, where she's going, or who these new people are, so you must do everything you can to make her feel comfortable as you begin your new life together.

THE KEY THING is to relax and not overthink things. Dogs are very adaptable and roll with things much better than we do, so odds are your new pup will take it all in stride. If she's never been in a car before or never really enjoyed it, it can be a strange experience. The best place to put her for the ride home depends on several factors, so you'll have to judge what's best. If your new dog is content in a crate, that might be the best place for her as it's a familiar place where she already feels comfortable.

I PREFER to have dogs secured with a seat belt when in the car, just like kids. There are special seat belt harnesses that limit them from moving around by the car's motion and keep them from being thrown forward if the driver brakes suddenly. While I like to have dogs in a seat belt, this first car ride home is a little different because you don't know what your new dog is accustomed to, so just use your best judgment whether to use a crate or a seat belt restraint. It's important to understand what your state requires by law, too. In many states, dogs must be secured in some way, either with a guard fence for the rear of larger vehicles, a crate, or a seat belt.

Take Your New Dog On A Tour

When you arrive home, take your new dog for a short walk around the neighborhood, weather permitting, to shake off the car ride and get to know the smells of her new area. Dogs use their noses to explore their world, and this is how they learn the most about their surroundings. Don't rush the walk —let her sniff and take in all the new sights, sounds, and smells. Walking anywhere from 5 to 15 minutes is good, but feel free to take longer if you'd like.

ONCE YOU'VE COMPLETED the walk, it's time to show your new pooch around the house. Keep her on the leash as you enter the house, or let her off leash but follow closely and walk with her around your house. Show her the entire house, even rooms that will be off-limits to her initially. Until dogs smell and learn about something, they have unfinished business. They like to investigate everything new and can't really move on until they've given everything a good sniff.

Show Your Dog Home Base

Once the tour is over, bring your dog to the place that will be her starting area, which is her home base. This can be a single room or a couple of rooms. Home base is where you will put her crate, bed, toys, and maybe her food and water bowls. Let her explore the area and spend some time with her in it. If she's still got some energy, play with her using some of her new toys. If she's a little tired after the journey home, let her rest while you sit nearby. Even though you may not interact directly, you're still starting the bonding process.

I RECOMMEND LEAVING a couple of toys and a bone or two within reach for her and putting the rest away. I rotate toys and bones occasionally to keep them fresh and exciting for my dog. If I want him to leave the carpet alone and give him a toy that he's been playing with all morning, it won't hold his interest. But if I take one of his standby toys he hasn't seen for a while out of the closet, he'll be excited and more likely to pay attention to it. Then I'll remove one of the toys that's been out for a while and put that one in the closet. This keeps everything fun and new so you can focus your dog's attention on appropriate things to play with (and keep her from chewing holes in your furniture.)

ONE LAST PIECE OF ADVICE: Don't invite many people to meet her right away. You just met her and didn't know much about her. Give her time to take in her new surroundings and learn to trust you and your family before you start throwing a bunch of strangers at her. I know you want to show her off to everyone, but remember, we want to set your dog up to succeed, so take it slow for a couple of weeks. Then, invite your friends over once you've gotten to know her better and know how she might react.

Dog Perspective

As I mentioned, dogs can be very much like kids, and like them, they go through successive developmental phases during which they have changing needs and can behave very differently. Here are some things to keep in mind depending on the age and stage of your new pup.

PUPPY

PUPPIES HAVE PRETTY MUCH ONLY one agenda: play, play, play (with the occasional nap thrown in.) They are looking for fun, often in the wrong places, and eager to explore and learn about their new environment. They often have bursts of activity followed by rest. In the beginning, periods of play will be fairly short, but play blocks will get longer as your dog ages.

BECAUSE EVERYTHING IS new to your puppy, it's your job to teach her what appropriate behavior looks like. Supervision is critical—you want to be there every step to teach your new pup what's expected of her and reduce the number of times she repeats undesirable behaviors. This is how you will help her form good habits instead of bad ones. Like a toddler, your puppy depends on you to help her grow into a well-mannered young adult.

ADOLESCENT (11 MONTHS to 3 Years)

HAVING A PUPPY CAN BE EXHAUSTING, and my clients tend to look back at the 10- or 11-month mark and say, "Oh, thank god, we survived puppyhood and now we can relax." Wrong. This is usually when things go a little sideways because they've survived having a puppy, but they've smacked face-first into having the dog equivalent of a teenager. Adolescent pups tend to think they know it all, forget what you taught them, and constantly push the boundaries.

NOT EVERY PUPPY will turn into a wild teenage dog, though. Some dogs will cruise through adolescence with ease. Most, however, will give you a little pushback during this time. This is actually when everyone calls me in for help. I would say that about 80 percent of the calls I get for behavioral problems are for adolescent dogs. Dogs might start barking even though they'd always been quiet, chew up stuff they never touched before, or blow off learned skills.

I RECOMMEND the most training during this phase because dogs need strong guidance to navigate adolescence. This is a great time to enroll your dog in a group obedience class, reinforce good behaviors, or add in more exercise. It's similar to how I keep my kids busy with lots of activities because if they don't have stuff to do, they will find stuff to do—and I might not like their choices.

ADULT (LARGE BREEDS: 2 to 7 Years; Small Breeds: 3 to 10 Years)

IF YOU'VE SPENT your training time wisely in your dog's puppy and adolescent periods, you'll be rewarded with a good dog as they become an adult. By now, most dogs will have matured out of many of the behaviors that plagued you when they were puppies. They will be less hyper, better at listening and calm down more easily and for longer periods. Although you may see a dip in their activity level, many high-energy dogs will still need plenty of exercise and stimulation throughout adulthood.

It is important to realize that no matter how hard you've worked along the way, no dog will ever be perfect. You should continue to help your dog with any trouble spots, but you also need to understand their personality and capabilities. I call it "the dog you want vs. the dog you have." You have this image of what the perfect dog acts like in your head. Then you have the dog you brought home, which most likely won't fit exactly into that mold. You can work to train him as best you can but recognize that there may be some things you can't change—and that's okay.

Love your dog for all his good qualities, but understand their personality and breed limitations. Spend time training him on the things you would like, but know that there may be some things you just have to accept and manage.

Senior (Large Breeds: 7 to 10+ Years; Small Breeds: 10 to 18+ Years)

As dogs age, their lifestyles change, which can sometimes be difficult for us to accept. I remember my pit bull, Hayley, used to love playing fetch in the swimming pool. I would throw the ball in the deep end, and she would cannonball into the water, grab it, and wait eagerly for me to throw it in again. She would do this for hours. Then one day, after playing in the pool, I noticed she was limping a bit and having some discomfort. At the time, she was about eight years old, and I realized that although we both loved playing aquatic fetch, it was time to retire from that activity.

THINGS YOUR DOG used to do may no longer be the safest choice for them, or your dog's preferences may change. You might see your dog moving more slowly on walks or opting to rest instead of running in the yard. Although it's sad, sharing your life with a dog is a natural part. Instead of being bummed out by everything you can no longer do, embrace this new chapter with your dog and enjoy snuggling on the couch and taking slow, meandering walks instead of high-impact activities. Just as it is for people, eating right and exercising regularly will help your dog transition into this time gracefully and with fewer complications.

RESCUE

MANY PEOPLE incorrectly assume that all rescue dogs come with behavior problems and are more of a challenge than a new puppy. The truth is that some dogs don't have homes because they had some issues, and people either couldn't or wouldn't work on improving them. However, so many dogs in shelters and rescues are there simply because there aren't enough homes or they encountered some bad luck, leaving them without someone to care for them. I've worked in rescue organizations and even ran my own for many years, and I can tell you that some truly amazing dogs are waiting to be adopted. Both of my dogs came from rescue organizations, and although I'm a bit biased, they're the best dogs in the world.

WHEN YOU BRING A RESCUED dog home, remember that you don't know what experiences she has had, what rules she was told to follow in her past (if any!), or what behaviors she's shaped over her lifetime. You need to get to know her a little bit to understand who she really is and where you need to focus your training. The first three to four weeks after you bring a dog into your home is what I call the "honeymoon period." You and your home are very new to your dog, and she's not sure whether this is temporary or she'll be sticking around for a while. Her behavior can be inhibited since she's not yet confident in her surroundings. After about a month, she will stretch out and say, "I'm home!" and feel comfortable being herself. At that point, you'll get a better picture of her behavior and what behaviors you might need to work on. Just be understanding and patient while you teach her your rules because they may differ from what she's experienced before.

5

CRATE TRAINING SUCCESS

N ow it's time to get to work and start teaching your new dog just how to live in this human world. Remember, if you don't show him how to behave, he's going to make it up on his own, which is sure to conflict with your preferences for indoor living. Luckily, your pup is super smart and very capable of figuring out what you ask of him. He'll be willing to do it your way if you properly show him what your rules are.

I'VE MAPPED out the skills in an order that I think is relevant for most dogs, putting those of higher importance first, but you can adjust them according to your own personal needs. As I mentioned earlier, it's best to only teach one new skill at a time. Then, as your dog gets the hang of each one, you can work on multiple things together over the following days and weeks. Try not to rush your dog too much, have patience as he figures things out, and keep in mind that every dog will progress at a different pace.

. . .

USING a crate is the best way to house-train your dog and keep him out of mischief while he's learning the rules of your home. Some people use a crate temporarily, while others keep it for their dog's entire life as their "room" (my three-year-old beagle loves his crate and still likes to nap there and sleep in it overnight). In the beginning, you may need to use the crate more than you would like because you won't be able to trust your dog to make good decisions just yet. As he learns what to do (and what not to do) and builds good habits, you'll be able to leave him out of the crate more often and eventually get rid of it entirely if you wish.

Great Crates

Crates come in a variety of sizes and materials. Like any product you can buy for your pooch, there is no one-size-fits-all option. You need to find the crate that works the best for you, your dog, and your environment. Here's a breakdown of some of the options available to you.

- **Wire crates:** The most common, least expensive, and most versatile crate on the market is the wire crate. Most come with a divider so you can get the size that would fit your dog once he's full grown. Use the divider to create a smaller space for him as a puppy and modify how big the area is as he grows. It's easy to clean and lightweight so you can transport it and move it throughout your house.
- **Plastic crates:** These are made of thick plastic and have less open space, so they create a more den-like environment that many dogs prefer. Plastic crates are a bit heavier and bulkier and don't come with anything to limit the interior size.

- **Flexible crates:** Made from nylon or other fabrics, these crates are lightweight and easy to carry with you when you're on the go. The downside is that they don't hold up as well and can be chewed, scratched up, and ripped open if a dog is motivated enough.
- **Wooden crates:** These are solid, well-constructed crates that resemble a piece of furniture. Some are even designed to look like an end table and are a great long-term option. They are not as easy to clean as the other crates on this list and not a good option for dogs that like to chew things.

The Goal

As I previously mentioned, the crate is a safe place where your dog can't get into trouble, and he innately doesn't want to pee and poop in there. Regardless of how old your dog is or where you got him from, your home and the stuff inside it are brand-new to him—he's never experienced these things in this way before. He'll have to learn what he's allowed access to, what is his, and what stuff is off-limits to him. That will take some time, so while you're teaching him all those things, you need a place to put him temporarily when you can't supervise him.

CRATES ARE NOT PRISON, and you're not putting your dog in there to punish him. All dog training should always be win-win and the crate is no exception. Most dogs are reluctant to be separated from the people they love and all that neat stuff in your house, but if you do things right, your dog should be fine with hanging out in his crate from time to time.

The Easy Method

The crate should be a nice, pleasant place for your dog where he can relax while you're away doing your own thing. If you do this right, not only will it be a place where you can leave him when you can't supervise, but it can also be a place that he chooses to go to when he wants to take a nap or needs some alone time (yes, dogs sometimes need this, too). It's basically his room—a place that's totally his, available to him at all times, and where he feels comfortable.

SINCE DOGS ARE VERY SOCIAL, if given the choice, your dog will probably prefer to be with you 24/7, but that's not healthy for either of you. His life will most likely include some time alone in the future and the sooner he gets used to it, the easier this process will be. So, even if you're home all the time, I recommend you get out of the house every now and then to get your dog used to being by himself occasionally.

SINCE STAYING in his crate by himself is not something your dog might initially choose to do, you need to sweeten the deal for him. Ultimately, you want him to like his crate so you don't have to force him to go there. Instead, he'll do so voluntarily. You will have to do three things to accomplish this. First, reward him for going into the crate and for doing lots of repetitions. Second, set aside yummy bones that he will only get in the crate, making it a special place. Third, only leave him inside for short periods at first, then slowly increase the time as he gets more comfortable.

STEP 1: Crate Shaping

. . .

CHOOSE some tasty treats that your dog loves. To make everything a win-win, remember: The less your dog wants to do something, the more you need to up his reward. If your dog doesn't have an aversion to the crate and is pretty food-motivated, you can use dry kibble or any treat. If he's already reluctant to go into the crate, choose something a little more motivating like freeze-dried liver or soft, meat-based treats. It should be something your dog likes and small enough that you can give him a bunch throughout the day without causing him to gain too much weight. You might have to experiment to see what is best for your dog.

ONCE YOU'VE DECIDED on the right treat, it's time to start building the repetitions. Take that yummy treat, put it right on your dog's nose, and lead him over to and inside the crate. Try to keep the treat right on his nose as you go, go slowly, and lure him inside the crate. Once he goes in, turn him around so he's facing the open door, give him his snack, and let him come back out. Do that for some time until he's happily and quickly going inside the crate to get his treat.

WHEN THAT'S GOING WELL, it's time to take it to the next level. Do the same thing, but this time after he turns around in the crate, close the door for only a second or two, open it back up, reward him, and let him out. Do some repetitions and then start to gradually increase the length of time he has to wait with the door closed before he gets his treat. Practice this throughout the day on and off as opposed to doing one long training session. Try a couple of reps, then a few more an hour later, and a few more sometime after that. Start out with having your dog go into and out of his crate 10 times per day.

IF YOU LIKE, once your dog is going in fairly easily, you can also attach a verbal cue to it. As you lead him to the crate, say the cue you want to use, like "Go to bed." Once he's going into the crate easily and waiting with the door closed for a few seconds, start to phase out the rewards. Instead of giving him a treat every time he goes into the crate, only give him a treat every other time. Do that for a length of time and then move to giving the food reward every third time and so on. No matter what, make sure you give him lots of verbal praise and affection every single time.

STEP 2: Long-Lasting Rewards

ASSUMING IT'S YUMMY ENOUGH, a treat will likely get your dog into the crate, but getting him to stay there for any period without complaint is another story altogether. Chances are that once your dog goes in and sees you leaving him, he'll want to come with you. This might cause him to voice his objections quite loudly. Remember everything should be a win-win, so you need to find a way to keep him happily busy while he's in the crate. You don't want your pooch upset during his crate time and I'm sure you don't want to feel guilty about having to leave him in there.

THE BEST WAY TO do this is to use food-based toys and bones that he loves and that take him some time to finish. He will need to be alone in his crate every now and then, so you will need to give him something that he'll have to work on for a bit and that you feel comfortable leaving him with unattended. This is why it's so important to supervise everything you give your dog to chew on in the beginning so you can make sure it's safe for him and see exactly how long it takes him to finish it.

BULLY STICKS and natural bones are good options, but my favorite choice is a frozen Kong toy (as mentioned in chapter two that is stuffed with something that your dog likes to eat. My go-to filling is simple peanut butter because I always have some in the house. You can also mix your dog's dry food with plain yogurt or canned pumpkin. Wet dog food is another simple choice that's easy to put in the Kong and freezes well. Feel free to experiment to see what keeps your dog's focus, what works best frozen, and what will take at least 15 minutes for him to get through. Once you figure out what your dog likes the best, only give it to him in the crate to make it a special place where great stuff happens.

STEP 3: Leaving Him for Longer Lengths of Time

Now that you've trained your dog to happily go into the crate whenever you ask him to and you've found some bones and/or Kong recipes that keep his interest, it's time to start leaving him alone. Start off by giving him some active exercise to drain his energy, put him in the crate with his favorite bone or a Kong, close the door, go to the next room for a few minutes, and see how he does. If he sticks with his chewing, you're good. Leave him alone for five minutes or so and then open the crate, take away his bone or Kong, and repeat later on.

· · ·

As you continue to do this, leave him for longer and longer and experiment with leaving the house completely. Over time, you will create the habit of your dog being calm, not paying attention to you while you leave, and just hanging out while you're away. Once you're doing really well and have been practicing this for a few weeks without incident, you can try to leave your dog in the crate without the bone or Kong. Again, make sure you tire him out with exercise first and start slow, only leaving him for a short time.

When you begin this whole process, if your dog starts whining or barking for more than just a few minutes when you leave the room, start by staying in the room where he's crated. Ignore him completely—read a book or scroll through your phone—and see if he settles down with the bone, content with the fact that you're still there. Do that for some time and then try to walk in and out of the room periodically to see how he responds. Hopefully, over time he'll get comfortable with being alone.

It's okay to leave him there even if he's making a little fuss (I know it's hard), but you have to wait it out and see if he'll eventually get used to the idea and settle down. If he's biting at the crate or looks like he might injure himself, let him out and contact a local dog behavior consultant/trainer to help you work on the issue safely.

6

POTTY TRAINING

I always prioritize house-training with any new puppy or newly adopted dog because, if done correctly, it can be completed in five to eight weeks, and then it's over. No, it's not fun, but if you put in the time and effort (and sleep a little less), you'll be done sooner and with a great dog to show for it. Remember, there are no shortcuts, and everyone who owns a puppy must undergo the same procedure. Some puppies are easy to train, while others are more difficult, but the process is always the same. Adult dogs who have never been trained and have a habit of going inside will require a little more time and patience. However, the procedure is the same regardless of the dog's age or history. The more you stick to the plan, the faster you can house-train your children.

The Goal

Your objective here is to ensure your home doesn't smell like a monkey enclosure at the zoo. You need to train your new dog to do all her business outside and to see your entire house as her den that she wants to keep clean. This may come as a shock, but no dog comes home innately knowing that she's supposed to go only outside. Your dog knows that if she feels like she has to go, there's no need to be uncomfortable if she can just go right where she is. However, dogs can learn fairly easily to only relieve themselves outside if you just shape it, so getting them in the right place at the right time is important.

IT'S ALL ABOUT REPETITIONS. You're trying to pile on lots of repetitions of going outside while limiting the number of accidents she has indoors. Over days and weeks of doing this successfully, the habit of only going to the bathroom outside will form. Although this is not the glamorous part of having a dog, you must prioritize it immediately so you can be done with it. Once that habit of only going outside sticks, you're done with this forever. Yeah!

THROUGHOUT THIS CHAPTER, I will use a puppy as an example, but the process is exactly the same for an older dog. Regardless of the dog's age, if it's not house-trained, I treat it like a puppy and go through the same steps. The only difference is that an older dog has a bigger bladder and can hold it for longer, which makes things a little less predictable. It also doesn't matter if you live in an apartment or a house, the process is still the same (just a bit trickier if you're on the top floor of a high-rise).

The Easy Method

I have great news for you: house-training your puppy is not rocket science. The system I use works 99 percent of the time if you can do what needs to be done and see it through.

Whenever I'm hired to work with an older dog that's not house-trained, it's always for one of two reasons: the owner didn't know what to do or knew but didn't want to do it. I know it's not necessarily fun, but it's part of being a responsible dog owner. If you put in the time and effort now, you'll get it over and done with sooner than you think.

Keep Your Dog's World Small

Giving your dog too much freedom is a surefire way to set her up to fail. I like to initially keep a dog's world small, then gradually expand it as she learns the rules. Too many people give their new puppy free rein of the house and then wonder why it smells like a urinal. Supervision is critical for house training and helping your dog learn how to live in this human world. You can only set her up to succeed if you show her exactly what you want her to do every step of the way.

I TALKED ABOUT THIS ALREADY, but you must first limit your new dog's access. Start her off in just a room or two by using gates or closing doors but with supervision. My rule is "Eyes on the dog at all times." When you have stuff to do, use the crate. It is the most powerful tool for house training because, if done correctly, it becomes a den where she will not want to pee or poop. The crate cannot be too large to serve as a den. It should be slightly larger than the dog. It cannot be so large that your dog can pee in one corner while sleeping in the other. As I mentioned in chapter two, large dog crates have dividers that should be used to make the crate smaller when the dog is a puppy and only expand the crate as the dog grows.

. . .

IF THE CRATE is the proper size for your puppy and she hasn't developed the habit of using it as her bathroom, it becomes your safe haven where you can put her and be sure she won't pee (typical of most dogs bought from a pet store).

IF YOUR DOG has been peeing and pooping in the crate, you might want to try feeding her in the crate. This increases the den-like atmosphere, and dogs don't want to pee where they eat.

The Right Place at the Right Time

Dogs don't usually know where to pee and poop. They will not learn unless you teach them. Total the amount of time your puppy spends outside in 24 hours. What does it add up to? It will be maybe two hours or so if you're like most people. That means that for two hours a day, your puppy can go to the bathroom in the right place, and for 22 hours a day, he has the opportunity to do it in the wrong place. Think about that for a minute. The odds of your puppy ever getting it right are minuscule—most of the time he's in the wrong place. You need to properly manage the 22 hours he spends inside so you can steer him to the right place effectively.

The Plan

The better organized you are, the less difficult this process will be. Here's how I'd organize a potty-training schedule for each day. Take your pup out of her crate first thing in the morning, assuming she hasn't gone to the bathroom in her crate overnight, and carry her (pick her up and don't let her feet hit the ground) outside to the same spot every time. Once she pees, praise her. I don't use treats because the timing has to be perfect, which few people can do, and all puppies love praise and affection. Then go back inside for a supervised free time. You can't fix what you don't see, so if you find a puddle but didn't see your puppy create it, simply clean it up and keep a closer eye on her.

IF YOU CATCH her in the act of going inside the house, make a noise (something like "Hey!") loud enough to startle her but not so loud that you scare her. Pick her up and take her outside. Odds are your puppy's little bladder has emptied already. However, if she finishes outside, throw a party for her.

THAT'S IT. That's all you do. Nothing more. No sticking her nose in it. No yelling or giving her a time-out.

A LITTLE WHILE AFTERWARD, it's probably time for breakfast and water. Puppies are extremely predictable: what goes in, comes out. And the younger the puppy, the more you can time it. If an eight-week-old puppy takes one sip of water, it will come out in about 10 minutes. The older the dog, the longer she can hold it, but if food or water goes in, you can be sure it will come out.

GIVE your puppy food and water, then wait anywhere from 10 to 30 minutes, depending on her age, and bring her outside again. Give her more supervised free time inside and commend her if she goes. This is effective for pee, but poop can be a little more difficult to predict. The majority of dogs will poop one more time per day than they will eat. So, a puppy fed three times per day will poop four times on average. Remember this especially if it's late in the day and your dog has only pooped once. Odds are, she will need to go, so keep bringing her outside. A good gauge to go by is that your puppy can hold it one hour per every month of age. That means a three-month-old dog can hold it in for about three hours. If you make her wait any longer, it's your fault if she has an accident. The exception to this rule is when she is inactive and not receiving food or water.

OKAY, back to the potty training. If you ever think, "I wonder if she has to go out?" take her out. It's impossible to take her out too much at this point. When in doubt, take her out. If she goes, praise her and allow more supervised free time. If she does not go, crate her when you get inside—even if you want to play with her. Please wait for 15 to 30 minutes and take her back outside. If she goes, she's allowed supervised free time; if she doesn't, put her back in the crate. Keep cycling her from crate to outside until she finally goes, at which point she's allowed more supervised free time. If she didn't go outside and you know she has to go soon, she needs to go into the crate where she innately doesn't want to pee or poop. This makes making a mistake extremely difficult for her. Most problems occur in house-training because the owners are not supervising, giving too much free water, or not using the crate correctly.

CONTINUE with this routine throughout the day: outside, pee, poop, praise, and then supervised free time. If she doesn't pee outside at any time, she goes back and forth from the crate to outside until she goes, then she's allowed free time. Before bedtime, please ensure you take your pup out for potty break.

I usually recommend no water after 8 p.m. to ensure a puppy's bladder is empty overnight. Then put your puppy to bed in her crate to sleep.

IF YOU HAVE a young pup (7 to 10 weeks of age), get up in the middle of the night to take her out again. You don't want her to pee in the crate because potty training gets very tricky if you lose the crate as your safe place. If a family member goes to bed late and another gets up early, experiment with letting the night owl handle that last pee before bed and letting the early bird make the first-morning trip. Its not possible really know what will work best for you and your puppy—just try out different things until something sticks.

ONE MISTAKE PEOPLE make with house-training is not to monitor water. If you take your pup out and she pees but takes a big drink of water when you come back into the house and you don't notice, she will pee again very soon. This is why supervision is so critical. You must understand exactly what is going into your puppy—and when—so you can take advantage of the times she probably has to go and get her in the right spot to do her business. You can either watch her all the time or don't leave water down all the time. Offer water at minimum with meals. You can also leave it out whenever you prefer during the day, but only give the amount you're comfortable with. Don't let your puppy drain the whole water bowl. Her bladder can only process so much at once, and she'll have to go every 20 minutes for an hour or so.

THE SECOND BIG mistake people make is bringing their puppy back inside before she has peed. You may take your dog out when it's time but she doesn't go right away. You might shrug your shoulders, thinking she must not have to go, and then bring her inside, where she promptly pees on the floor. The problem here is that, yes, your dog did have to go, but once outside, she got distracted by a butterfly or a blowing leaf and forgot why she went out there. When she got back inside without the distractions, she realized, "Oh yeah, I've got to pee." To combat this, send her right to the crate every time your puppy doesn't go outside.

REMEMBER, you're not punishing her. Give your puppy her favorite bone or a stuffed Kong to make her feel happy. Bring her outside again in 15 to 30 minutes and keep repeating this process until she eventually pees outside. Then give her supervised free time.

Long-Term Confinement

If you have to leave your puppy alone for longer than she can realistically hold it in, you don't want to leave her in a small crate where she'll be forced to sit in her pee. That's unfair to her and will create some bad habits. If you have to leave for extended periods, you should either hire a dog walker or create a long-term confinement area. If possible, put your puppy in a pen or small room with the open crate on one side and some pads or newspaper on the other side directly opposite the crate. Dogs prefer to go as far away from their sleeping place as possible.

Why I Don't Like Wee-Wee Pads

Wee-wee pads seem logical to use in your home if you can't get your dog out in time. At least he's going on the pads and not your floor, right? Unfortunately, using them will undermine your house-training process, confuse your dog, and make house-training take so much longer (it may even foil the whole thing). Using wee-wee pads teaches your dog that it's occasionally okay to go in the house, and you don't want to reinforce that habit. Don't forget about those pesky repetitions. The more your dog pees and poops in your house, the more likely he will continue down that path.

YES, it's more convenient for you to just let your pup use the pads instead of going outside in the rain and cold and in the middle of the night, but you're only hurting yourself by doing it. If you can stick to the system and make some sacrifices now, you can be done with it. I've never met a pad-trained dog that hit the mark 100 percent of the time. They all miss and make mistakes because to them, there's very little difference between a pad and your rug. Some dogs will do pretty well with the pad in their home, but they will not know the difference elsewhere because their habit is only in their house.

SO, invest now, put in the effort, and keep your home pee-free.

7

LEASH TRAINING

W hen you first considered getting a dog, you probably imagined long walks around your neighborhood on a beautiful sunny day. You probably didn't expect it to be an arm-jarring, hold-on-for-life drag. Before you get upset with your dog, remember that dogs are not programmed to walk the way we do. Walking like humans is extremely unnatural for dogs.

YOUR DOG IS THINKING, "Why aren't we running?" It just makes no sense to them to go so slow. "Why would you walk in a straight line when there are so many awesome smells all around you?" they wonder." Don't forget your dog's nose is exponentially more powerful than yours, and an overwhelming number of interesting scents are pulling at his sniffer, enticing him to investigate. It's as if you were walking down the street and saw what appeared to be hundred-dollar bills all over the place. It's as if you were walking down the street and saw what appeared to be hundred-dollar bills all over the place.

. . .

EVEN THOUGH WALKING in a straight line next to slow humans goes against everything canine, your dog can be trained to tolerate and accept your pace. However, it is only possible with time and practice.

The Goal

Some people will argue that the dog should always be by your side or only on your left side, but I'm afraid I have to disagree. It doesn't matter if your dog is in front of you, behind, or to the side, as long as you're showing him or doing competitive obedience and the leash is relaxed. It's best to have a large and strong dog on your dominant side to give you a little more strength.

YOU'LL NOTICE that I don't include anything about teaching your dog to stay right by your side in this chapter. That's not an oversight. It's very intentional. I don't teach heel. I don't want a robot dog that sticks to my side like glue—that's taking the dog out of the dog. Instead, I like dogs to enjoy the walk by taking in some of the magnificent scents that they pass. Instead of the heel, I prefer loose-leash walking. It doesn't matter if your dog is in front, behind, or off to the side as far as the leash is relaxed, assuming a six-foot lead.

THE IDEAL LEASH is not tight. If the leash is tense, so is the dog, and he is unaware of the cause of the tension. Often, a dog will project that tension at whatever is directly in front of him, generally people or other dogs.

The Easy Method

When teaching loose-leash walking, there are several approaches you can take. Keep in mind that what works for you may not work for someone else in your family. Here are a few techniques I typically employ when working with dogs who pull on a leash.

Stopping

This one is straightforward. When your dog pulls forward, and there is tension on the leash, simply stop and wait for him to transition from a forward to a neutral orientation. Whenever there is some slack in the leash, move forward again. It is an excellent technique because it is simple to execute. However, it may take some time for your dog to figure it out, and younger, high-energy dogs may struggle.

Changing Direction

When your dog moves ahead, and you feel the leash tightening, turn 180 degrees and go in the opposite direction, pulling him with you. If he pulls in the opposite direction when he catches up to you, turn around and pull him back in the opposite direction.

THESE ARE KNOWN AS "SWITCHBACKS." The dog will begin to look up at you, waiting for you to change direction again. And he can't be pulling if he's looking at you.

WHEN I VOLUNTEERED AT A SHELTER, I used this technique. The dogs were so excited to be outside that they would pull my arm off whenever we went for a walk. I'd start them in the alley outside the shelter and do about five minutes of these switchbacks to get their attention.

ONE EFFECTIVE VARIATION of this technique is to let your dog walk ahead of you. Immediately there is tension in the leash, call him and walk backward. Have a smelly treat in your hand, call him to you, and when he's within arm's reach, lure him in close and give him the food. Then continue your walk, repeating this process as you go. With time and repetition, your dog will begin associating the tension on the leash as a cue to return and get a snack.

Walk and Train

Giving your dog some tasks to keep his mind occupied on your walks is an excellent way to keep him from being distracted by the world and pulling you all over the place. For example, have him sit every 20 feet or so. Simply come to a halt and ask your dog to sit before rewarding him with a treat. Depending on where you're walking, you can do this every few feet or use landmarks like driveways as places to sit. Soon, he'll start anticipating the sits and will keep looking up at you to see if it's time for another. Simple sits are fine, but on walks, you can have him do all sorts of things to keep his attention. Use the walks as a training opportunity, and ask him to perform a variety of obedience skills or tricks.

YOU CAN EVEN USE the environment you're walking in to teach him "urban agility," such as climbing stairs, jumping rocks, and going around trees. Make it fun by using your imagination.

Teaching a Watch Cue

Teaching your dog a "watch" cue will enable you to ask for it frequently on walks, and he won't pull ahead if he's looking at you. This is an excellent tool for dogs who are easily distracted and enjoy chasing squirrels and birds, as well as dogs who are reactive to other dogs. Start teaching watch in your home without distractions and make some noise to get his attention. Every time he looks at you, reward him with a treat. Wait for him to look away and repeat. He will learn that he will receive a treat if he looks at you when you make a sound. Isn't that cool? Once he always looks at you when you make a noise, stop making the noise and say "watch" (or whatever word you want) instead.

AFTER YOU'VE MASTERED it inside with no distractions, start practicing with mild distractions, like if he hears something outside but is not reacting to it. Then, once he's good with that, try it outside without distractions and start piling on repetitions. It will take some time to get good repetitions, but it is so powerful.

Using a Training Collar/Harness

If your dog excessively pulls on the leash, you might want to experiment with some different tools to help you work with him on leash walking. However, remember that the tool should only be used to supplement your training, not as a replacement. Too many people depend on the tool and never get off it.

. . .

A FRONT-ATTACHING harness is one of my favorites for medium or large dogs. Instead of being attached to the dog's back like a standard harness, it connects in front at the chest. The cool thing about this type of harness is that it self-corrects—when your dog pulls, he gets turned around in the opposite direction. When this happens, hold the leash and wait for him to pull; he'll calm down once he realizes he's not going anywhere.

YOU CAN EXPERIMENT with various leashes, harnesses, and collars. Remember that every dog is unique, and it may take some trial and error to find the right tool for you.

AS YOU WORK with your dog on his leash-walking skills, remember that teaching your dog to walk like a human is not something that comes naturally to him. You'll need to give him some time and practice for it to take effect. Younger energetic dogs that are very distractible will have a harder time focusing when out for a stroll. I know it may seem counterintuitive, but if you exercise your dog before you go for a walk, he'll be more likely to pay attention to you.

ANOTHER THING TO keep in mind is that the beginning of your walks will always be more challenging because your dog is excited to be outside and is fired up to take in all the different stimuli around him. So please do your best to manage it in the first half of the walk, and once your dog has burned off some of the initial energy and has gotten used to being outside, work on leash walking more. Remember that if you have a high-energy breed, you'll probably have to walk for at least 20 minutes to bring his energy level down.

8

SOCIALIZING YOUR DOG

Most clients call me because of behavior problems with their adolescent or adult dogs. These dogs are typically between the ages of one and three, and the behaviors have usually been present for some time before the clients contact me.

IN NEARLY ALL CASES, the problem stems from a lack of socialization. You need to be proactive and try to socialize your dog as much as possible, starting as soon as possible. So many dogs do not get the valuable socialization needed to become accustomed to the world around them and resilient to new experiences because people don't really understand what true socialization is, and it doesn't seem urgent until it's too late.

The Goal

True socialization entails acquainting and reassuring your dog about everything in our human world. I like your furry friend to have a "been there, done that" attitude so that no matter where you go, he will roll with what's thrown at him. The three big things to concentrate on concerning socialization are people, dogs, and environments. They will impact just about every dog's (and their human's) life, and they must be addressed greatly.

I BELIEVE that socialization should start as soon as you bring your dog home, but precautions should be taken to ensure it's done safely and effectively. You want to make sure that everything is either a positive or neutral event. To do that, it's important to stack the deck in your favor by creating controllable situations where you can show your dog how wondrous the world is and that there's nothing to fear or be anxious about. A dog can be socialized at any age, but the longer you wait, the older the dog is, and the harder and more time-consuming the process can be. It's best not to delay.

The Easy Method

At its core, socialization is simply getting your dog out into the world and allowing him to see everything that's going on. The more experiences and encounters he has that go well, the more he'll be okay with changes in the future. If your dog is secluded in your house and yard and never gets a chance to see anything outside its confines, your home is the only place he'll ever feel comfortable. I'd like for you to be able to take your dog anywhere, for him to love everyone, and be able to interact with any dog. This doesn't happen on its own, though. Ensure you expose your dog to all kinds of people, dogs, and environments, so they're familiar to him. This is how he will gain the confidence to make him more stable when unexpected stimuli cross his path.

. . .

LET'S examine each of the big three areas you need to socialize your new dog so you understand how to do it effectively.

Socialization with People

You want your dog to love everyone, so you don't have to worry about her being anxious or aggressive with the people in your life. To do this, you need to expose your dog to many people. How many people would you say is a good number? Forget it, don't even guess. I guarantee your guess would be way less than what is required. Just get your dog in front of as many people as possible.

DON'T GET TOO STRESSED out by the numbers—just do the best you can and know that more is undoubtedly better. You also need to introduce your pup to all different kinds of people, every race and ethnic group, every height and body type, old and young, people wearing glasses and hats, people carrying umbrellas, people on crutches and using canes and in wheelchairs, people wearing Halloween costumes, Santa Claus, people in winter coats and wearing brightly colored rain jackets, people on roller skates and scooters and skateboards, people, people, people.

ALLOW all these people to interact with and handle your puppy, but keep an eye on everything. All these encounters must be positive experiences for your dog, or you'll be headed in the wrong direction. Most puppies will be thrilled with the attention, but keep a close watch on your dog's body language and recognize when you should give her a reprieve from all those reaching hands.

BE ESPECIALLY careful during interactions with children who often tend to be overcome by the cuteness of dogs. Their innocent enthusiasm can be a little too intense for your dog and cause her to become wary of children. Also, most dogs don't like people in their faces, so ensure everyone respects your dog's feelings and does not crowd her too much. If your dog looks uncomfortable with the attention at any time, give her the space she needs by moving people away for a bit.

Socialization with Other Dogs

All of the preceding guidelines also apply to socialization with dogs. Allowing your dog to sniff three butts per week on your weekly walks around the block is simply not enough. Always remember that dog socialization is done off leash so dogs can interact naturally. This is especially important for puppies who must develop bite inhibition, which is learning that the pointy teeth he has inside his mouth can hurt other dogs. If you watch two well-socialized adult dogs playing, you'll notice that they're constantly mouthing each other yet never hurt each other with all those teeth. When they were puppies, they did the same endless mouthing, but they would bite a little too hard every time. The other dog would yelp, then both dogs would stop playing and look at each other. The dog that chomped down a little too hard would realize that if he wanted to keep playing—and he did—he had to pull his punches.

. . .

THAT'S why puppy teeth are shaped like little pointy needles: to teach the puppy that biting hurts and to give him a nice soft mouth. Because some puppies can put up with a lot of inappropriate biting, you must socialize your puppy with older dogs as well.nOlder dogs will tolerate a lot of mistakes from puppies but will also make corrections to teach them what's appropriate and what's not. And when they do correct the pup, they do it gently because they know he's just a kid who doesn't know any better. If a puppy doesn't learn when he is young and makes the same mistakes as an adolescent, the older dogs may not be as kind.

FOR THIS REASON, you need to be more cautious when first letting adult dogs interact. Your dog might not have learned the proper manners, and if the dog he's playing with is not tolerant, there can be trouble. Try to find well-socialized, very friendly dogs to be playmates. Then, as you get an idea of how well your dog plays and interacts with other dogs, you can start experimenting with other dogs you don't know.

Socialization with the Environment

The environment is the next stop on your path to socialization enlightenment. The human world is full of strange places, noises, contraptions, and events, and unless a puppy learns about these things, he may become terrified when exposed to them as an adult. However, if he has witnessed it all from a young age, he will learn that all this strange stuff in the human world will not harm him.

IT'S as if you woke up this morning to find a UFO in your backyard. I'm sure it would make you feel a little uneasy (a change of underwear may even be in order). But if you'd previously seen UFOs and nothing bad had happened, you'd probably be fine with it.

EVERYTHING A DOG SEES for the first time is a UFO to him. If a one-year-old dog has never seen a moving train and one passes by making all that noise, he will panic. Consider how terrifying an experience it would be if you had no idea what it was. So, you need to expose your dog to everything this human world has to throw at him. Even if you live nowhere near a train and have no plans of ever being around one, try to find one and let your puppy experience it. You never know where life will take you. But if you try to expose your dog to everything, you can be confident that he'll adapt easily.

START with things in his everyday life and then move on to the more unusual and obscure. Begin in your home with every appliance and gadget you own: dishwasher, coffee maker, hair dryer, garbage can, camera, fans, umbrellas, and anything and everything else you can think of. Then hit the road and show your dog the world: the bank, the groomer, fireworks, cars, trucks, buses, planes, rivers, the ocean, bicycles, skateboards, in-line skates, scooters, parades, concerts, big cities, large crowds, subways, and whatever else you can expose him to.

ONE POINT TO remember is that all of these experiences need to be either positive or a nonevent. It's natural for your dog to be suspicious of something he hasn't seen before. Keep him near it until he realizes that, while it may appear frightening and make loud noises, it will not harm him. Take care not to overburden your dog. Recognize when a situation may provide too much stimulation or be too intense for him. For something like a train, you should start a good distance away from the tracks and slowly move closer as your dog adjusts.

The Truth About Dog Parks

Dog parks seem like canine nirvana in theory, but they are very flawed in application. I believe dog parks are gambles where you make a lot of assumptions. You assume that every dog is healthy. That is not always the case. You assume that every dog is friendly. Nope. And you assume every person there is responsible. Very unlikely. With the perfect mix of people and dogs, dog parks are great places where your dog can play, socialize, and just be a dog. The problem is that it only happens about 10 percent of the time.

HERE ARE my recommendations on using dog parks safely. First, don't go at peak times like weekend afternoons or after work. The busier it is, the more energy there will be swirling around, and the more likely trouble will arise. The best times to go are off-hours, where you get some regulars that all know one another. My second tip is to hang out and watch the action in the dog park for about a minute before you enter. Look at the dogs and the energy of the pack. Do you feel comfortable with what's going on? Take a look at the people, as well. Are they paying attention to the dogs or staring down at their phones? If, after a minute, you feel good about the group, go on in. If not, just go for a walk. And once you're in the dog park, if one dog or person enters that you don't feel good about, it's time to leave.

9

TEACHING BASIC COMMANDS

I'll cover five commands in this chapter: sit, down, stay, come, and wait. You can teach your furry buddy many other things, but just focusing on these will likely set you up with a solid foundation. Once your dog has learned these core skills, you can make them more challenging by working around distractions and adding more complex tasks to challenge her and build on her abilities. Learning other skills is great for you and your dog, but it's unnecessary after you've completed teaching the five essentials. You will decide what you feel is needed and what you want to do for yourself and your dog.

The Basics of Training Commands

To teach your dog a behavior she has never done before, you must first lure her into the position. Take a treat and put it close to, or sometimes directly on, her nose, but do not release it. Then move your hand, holding the treat, to lure her into the desired position. If your treat elicits enough motivation, her nose should stay glued to it, allowing you to control and position her as she follows the lure of the treat.

Once you are consistently luring your dog into the position, then and only then do you introduce the verbal aspect of the command. You don't say the command right at the beginning because your dog doesn't know what it means. Constantly repeating the command will only devalue it and get your dog in the habit of ignoring it. So, please wait until your dog is repeatedly doing the desired behavior easily with the lure, then add the verbal command to it.

I like teaching verbal commands and a hand signal for most basic cues. Dogs respond better to hand signals because they are more attentive to observing body language than verbal communication. It's nice to teach both, though, because it allows for more versatility in different situations. I use hand signals almost exclusively, but I need verbal signals when I'm out of the visual range of my dog.

Once your dog knows a particular command, you should phase out the lure. This is where many dog owners mess up by forgetting to get rid of the food. They then need to bribe their dogs to persuade them to do anything. As soon as your dog consistently does the desired behavior, only reward her with food intermittently. For example, she will get a treat every other time, third time, fourth time, tenth time, and so on. Giving intermittent rewards is much more powerful than rewarding every time. It's like playing a slot machine: Over time, a person only wins on about 1 out of every 50 pulls, but the possibility of that one win keeps them pulling the lever the other 49 times. Remember, when you're not giving her the food reward, you should always give plenty of verbal praise to assure her that she still did something cool.

THERE IS a big difference between a bribe and a reward. A bribe is when your dog will only do something if she sees a treat. A reward, however, comes out of nowhere and could appear whenever your dog does something right. In addition to rewarding intermittently, it's also important that the treats go out of sight. As soon as your dog knows the behavior, hide the reward and only bring it out after she has done what you've asked. Too many people keep holding onto the treats and form the bad habit of having to depend on them for compliance.

HERE'S how the sequencing looks for teaching a new skill:

1. Lure your dog into the desired position (what you want) using a small treat without saying anything.
2. Once you're luring your dog into the position successfully and consistently, add the verbal cue you want to associate with the behavior (for example, "sit").
3. Remove the lure. Say the command first, then after your dog complies, take the treat out and give it to her.
4. Phase out the treat. Start rewarding intermittently, only giving a treat every second or third time.

You want to say the verbal command and give the hand signal only once for most commands and tricks. If the dog knows what you're asking and she's still looking at you, wait.

She will almost always (eventually) do it. Getting your dog accustomed to you repeating the command over and over again devalues the command and tells your dog she only has to do the desired behavior on the tenth ask or whenever she feels like it. So, say it once and wait. Keeping eye contact and being confident that your dog understands your command will help her comply. When she does, reward her. She'll soon learn that the quickest way to earn a treat is to comply ASAP.

The Goal

Whatever breed of dog you have or your personal training goals, every dog and person benefits from learning the basic core skills. Teaching them to your dog will enhance your communication and help her understand how you want her to behave in your world. Once you've mastered this handful of cues, you can decide what you really need in the long term and what you would like to add to your dog's vocabulary.

Sit

Learning to "sit" begins with a treat right at the nose.

As soon as she sits, please give her a treat.

Consider sit to be the home button on your cell phone. When you need to get organized or things don't go as planned (settle your dog), hit the home button and reset. There's so much you can do with a simple sit, and it's the easiest and most useful skill you can teach your dog. If you're having trouble with your dog's behavior at any time in the future, have her sit and reset her. It's a great way to get her focus back onto you and open for direction. In the day-to-day life of a dog, a lot is going on and much to be distracted by. All dogs occasionally need a moment to settle and refocus their attention. That's what sit will do.

THE SIT COMMAND is the easiest to teach and will become every dog's go-to move—when in doubt, sit.

HERE ARE the steps to teach sit:

1. Take a treat and place it on your dog's nose, but don't let her eat it.
2. Move your hand up and just over her head, making sure you don't go too fast or move your hand too far away from her, which will cause her to follow the lure and jump up.
3. As your dog follows your hand's movements, her eyes will look up, and her butt will go down in her effort to keep her eyes and nose on the treat. If she backs up instead of sitting, just lure her back with the food and try again.
4. The second her butt touches the ground, release her food reward.

BREED CONSIDERATIONS

FOR DOGS WITH A DOCKED TAIL, like Dobermans and boxers, sitting can be uncomfortable, so it may be easier for them to do a down instead. Or instead of sitting straight, they can sit leaning to one side, which will be more comfortable. Experiment with your dog and see what she feels most comfortable with.

IF YOUR DOG moves backward while you're teaching sit, try doing it with your dog against a wall. If your dog is not doing it after several failed attempts, you can gently apply light pressure to her backside while you lure her with the treat.

ONCE YOUR DOG knows the basic "sit" command, slowly remove the lure and push the envelope a little. Too many people only practice sit while standing directly in front of their dog and can't get it from any other position. While walking, for instance, it's inconvenient to always have to turn and face your dog to get a sit. Practice sit facing the same direction as your dog when walking. You can then ask your dog to do it while sitting in a chair and, finally, while lying down (this is very hard because most dogs just want to jump on you and play).

Down

A treat at the nose also comes in handy for teaching your dog "down."

DOWN IS a great position for excitable, hyper dogs because it forces them to be still, which helps shift them into a calmer state of mind. I like to start teaching down on a tile or hardwood floor because the surface is somewhat slippery and can help slide a dog down as I'm luring. That being said, I've also worked with some dogs that refused to do it on the hard floor, but as soon as I moved them to a carpeted area, they went right down. Start on hardwood or tile; if you're not getting anywhere, experiment on a surface with more traction.

HERE ARE the steps to teach down:

1. With your dog in a sit, place the treat on her nose and move your hand directly down between her front paws, keeping the treat right on her nose. Many people will move the treat slowly away from their dog at an angle instead of going straight down, forcing the dog to follow the lure, break the sit, and move forward. So, make sure you slowly move the treat directly down, under your dog's head, then between her front paws.

2. Once your hand is on the ground with your dog's nose, hold it there without releasing the treat. Let your dog nibble on the treat while you slowly move your hand along the floor away from her.

THE KEY IS to move very slowly. When working with a little dog, I sometimes move toward the dog or go slowly back and forth instead of moving the lure away.

3. Your dog should slide down as you move the treat away from her nose, making her stretch her body out in front of her.

. . .

I<small>T SOUNDS EASY</small>, but this can take some time for stubborn dogs. If they stand up at any time, reset them and start again. Be patient. You might have to just let your dog nibble on the treat for a while as she's leaning down, waiting for her to get uncomfortable, so she chooses to go down.

4. As soon as your dog gets her upper body to the floor, release the food reward to her.

B<small>REED</small> C<small>ONSIDERATIONS</small>

D<small>OWN IS</small> a little trickier for some dogs, especially little dogs (such as dachshunds) with short legs, since they are already practically down, making them impossible to lure into the position. If you've got one of these stubborn downers, forget luring and just wait for them to eventually lie down on their own (at any time during the day) and reward them. After several repetitions, they may start to understand that lying down is something you like, and it will score them something yummy.

Stay

You'll use your voice and hand to direct your dog to "stay."

T<small>HE STAY COMMAND</small> means you want your dog to remain in exactly the same spot until you release her. I suggest you start teaching stay with your dog in a sit since that's probably her favorite position, and it is also the easiest command.

However, some dogs favor the down position, so you can start with a down/stay command.

Here are the steps to teach stay:

1. Put the dog in a sit or down position, put your flat hand in front of her in the stop sign position, and say, "Stay." (Stay is one of the commands that breaks my rule of not attaching a verbal command until the behavior has been shaped. With stay, you can start using the verbal cue right from the beginning.)

2. Wait a few seconds and give your dog a treat. Initially, you are not moving back at all. As you give your dog the treat, say "Okay" or whatever release word you choose. A release word indicates that your dog can now do whatever she wants. You give the release word as you're releasing the food because even if she breaks the sit at that point, which is common, you want her to think it was your idea.

3. Repeat the above steps. This time, after you give the command, move one foot back, keeping the other foot in place with your hand in front of you in the stop sign position. Wait a few seconds, reward, and release.

4. Next, give the command with the hand signal and move both feet back. Pause a few seconds, reward, and release.

. . .

5. Slowly increase distance and duration as your dog improves. Don't rush through this—ensure you're giving your dog enough time at each step, slowly building up her comprehension of what you want. Most dog owners try to move too quickly, but you must go at your dog's pace and only move to the next step after she has mastered the previous one. Remember, every dog will progress at their own pace.

STAY IS one of the only commands that can be repeated verbally over and over as needed. If your dog looks like she might break the stay, you can repeat it to remind her that you're not done yet. However, try to use it only as much as is really needed.

Come

Teaching your dog to "come" to you involves just a few simple steps.

IF YOU'RE ONLY GOING to teach one thing to your dog, it should be to come when called. Every single dog should not only learn the come command but become an expert at it because it's the single command that could save a dog's life one day. I'm always surprised at how stunned dog owners are when their dogs are reluctant to come to them after spending so little time practicing recall. If your dog ever gets loose and decides to run across the street to visit your neighbor, you'll be thankful you practiced the come cue. I know this all too well because I live on a very busy street and two dogs have been hit by cars in front of my house. You need to have a good

solid recall to be confident walking your dog around the
world's many distractions.

TEACHING come is contrary to the way we teach many of the
other commands. I recommend being calm and saying the
verbal command slowly and confidently for most of the other
commands. However, everything changes with come. This is
the time you want your dog a little fired up and excited. I
don't even use the word "come." Instead, I try to get a dog
excited by making myself as interesting as possible so that
she really wants to come over to me and see what is so fun.

HERE ARE the steps to teaching your dog to come when
called:

1. Start with your dog across the room and, in a high-pitched,
excited voice, call your dog over to you.

2. As soon as you get eye contact from your dog, squat down a
bit, clap your hands, and walk backward a step or two as you
continue to call her over to you.

3. As she approaches, keep her focus on you by continuing to
encourage her.

4. When she's within arm's reach, put a treat on her nose (but
don't give it to her yet) and lure her in close to your body.

. . .

5. With the treat still on her nose, gently grab her collar and release the food.

IT IS HARDWIRED into a dog's DNA to chase receding objects, so by moving backward after getting your dog's attention, she will start moving toward you without even being aware of it. If your dog is moving toward you, she gets distracted and looks away, up your excitement to get her focus back on you. At home in your living room, a simple come may do the trick, but the more distractions there are, the more you need to up your level of encouragement.

GETTING your dog to come in close and grabbing the collar at the end of the sequence are very important techniques because when you really need to use the come command, it's going to be a safety issue, and you'll want to be able to grab hold of her. You want your dog to know that the only way to get her reward is to come in close and feel your hand on her collar. Many dogs are very good at coming over to you while staying just out of reach as they determine if you have any food.

A BIG MISTAKE people make is to only call their dog to take her away from an object or situation or when they want to discipline her. Calling your dog over to you always needs to have a positive connotation, and you should never call your dog for anything negative. If you have to correct, you should go to her instead.

Pooch Perspective

. . .

MANY PEOPLE with fenced-in yards hire me because their dog won't come in from the backyard when called. You have to understand your dog's point of view here. If you only call your dog when you want to bring her inside away from all the fun, why would she ever come? Dogs are always thinking, "What's in it for me?" In this situation, it's really not in your dog's best interest to come inside.

YOU NEED to call your dog often when she's in the backyard, and 90 percent of the time just give her a yummy treat and then let her go back to having fun in the yard. You should bring her inside only 1 out of 10 times you call her. This way, it's a win-win for your dog—most of the time she's called, gets a surprise snack, and still gets to go back to having his fun in the yard. Those are odds she'll play all day long.

YOU CAN ALSO GRADE her performance by offering three different levels treats, depending on how quickly she comes. If she strolls over to you reluctantly, she gets a piece of dry dog food. If she comes over at a slight trot, she gets freeze-dried liver. And if she bolts to you like a rocket, she gets a piece of chicken. I like to use better-than-average treats for teaching recall since it's such an important command and you're likely to be facing some decent-level distractions outside when you really need it.

Wait

The "wait" command can be trained in just three easy steps.

. . .

WAIT IS the skill I use the most with my dog. It's similar to stay but less strict. Wait just means "Hang on a second," unlike stay, which can last for many minutes if necessary. Stay means "Stay exactly as I put you" (for example, if I have my dog do a down/stay and he sits up, he failed the command). But when doing a wait, he can sit down, get up, move from side to side—anything he wants except move forward. I use wait so much because it's the most applicable to everyday life. I have my dog wait for his food, before we go out the door, before we go down the stairs so he doesn't trip me by darting in front of me, and countless other times throughout our day together. It's a momentary thing that my dog knows will not take too long.

TEACHING wait is not about luring your dog; it's actually more about just doing lots of repetition until she figures it out.

HERE ARE the steps to teaching wait:

1. Have your dog on a leash and drop a low-motivating object a few feet away from her (with you in between her and the object). Something like a carrot usually works well. Ensure your dog is far enough away so she's not tempted to bolt for it right away but close enough that she can see it.

2. As soon as the object hits the ground, say "Wait" and hold up one finger (my hand signal for wait) in front of her.

. . .

3. Repeat the word "wait" a couple of times, then say "Okay" (or whatever release word you like) and encourage her to go investigate the object.

As your dog gets good, you can work with more motivating items, which can come in handy while cooking. I mistakenly dropped chocolate on the floor, which, as I mentioned, can be life-threatening to dogs, but my wait command kept my dog from moving toward it. Don't forget all the things I discussed in chapter one. If she's just not getting it or her compliance isn't where you would like it to be, it's likely that one or more of those key points are off. As with everything you do with your dog, be patient, don't rush, and have fun!

10

PREVENTING UNWANTED BEHAVIORS

No matter how much training you do or how amazing your dog is, you're bound to experience some behavioral issues with your new dog. Remember, you've invited a canine into your home who, although domesticated (and super cute), is still an animal and will tend to act pretty much like a dog. All behavior problems are just dogs acting like dogs. It's natural and to be expected. With time and effort, your dog will learn how you like things to be in the human world and will adapt their behavior to fit yours, even though it seems very strange to him. So, as you work through any of the following issues and more, remember that it's not personal—it's just your dog acting like a dog.

IF YOU'RE DOING your job of helping your dog understand your rules and what he needs to do (or not do) to fit into your family well, your dog's behavior should be improving every day. Along your journey, you'll undoubtedly need to address one or two or even five problem areas with your poochy pal.

Don't get too mad at him as he makes some mistakes, even though he may have just taken a few bites out of your favorite chair. He's really unaware that what he's doing is wrong and often just can't help his canine tendencies from coming out every now and then. Your dog is very trainable and can learn how to turn those problem behaviors around and be the good dog you want.

LET's troubleshoot some very common behavioral issues and how you can work to improve them.

Jumping On You or Other People

Jumping is a very common concern for dog owners because it's an excitement behavior, and as a general rule, dogs are lovers of life and have a tendency to get easily worked up around people. Your dog yearns to be with you and loves you, so it's natural for him to try to move up toward your face to get attention and perhaps a few face licks.

TYPICALLY, dogs jump because they want attention, and jumping usually forces people to address them. If attention is the reward, not giving your dog attention is a punishment, according to your dog. If jumping gets your dog's attention, why would he stop? But if jumping is not rewarded and having four paws on the floor is rewarded instead, your dog will do it every time. Immediately the light bulb goes off in your dog's head that the quickest way to his reward is keeping his paws on the ground; he will keep them planted every time.

. . .

THE EASY METHOD

THE IGNORING TECHNIQUE, although simple, works really well. Most people fail to realize that eye contact is a reward as well. No eye contact should be given, and energy should be kept as low as possible. Just look up and slowly turn your back to your dog every time he jumps up, and he'll quickly realize that this behavior is getting him nowhere fast. He's not getting what he wants, and after trying it unsuccessfully a few times, he should settle and end up looking up at you with those don't-you-love-me? eyes. You can reach down and greet him as soon he's got four paws on the floor and is calmer. If he jumps up again, go back to ignoring him again. If you're consistent, it won't take long for your dog to figure out that you'll engage with him quickly if he doesn't jump.

IF FOR SOME REASON, you're having trouble with that technique (big dogs are not so easy to ignore when they're climbing on top of you) or it's not working as you would like, there is another approach you can take. You know what you don't want your dog to do, so why not teach him exactly what you want him to do? For this, I like to play a little game I call "making sit happen."

LET'S use the example of you coming home, and your dog is so worked up upon seeing you that he's jumping as soon as you open your front door. Have some yummy treats ready, preferably ones with a lot of scents to them, like freeze-dried liver or a soft meat-based treat. As your dog charges over to you, have the treat out, so it meets his nose as he reaches you, put him into a sit, and give him the treat. Then immediately put another treat on his nose, lead him five feet ahead and have him do another sit. Then move him five more feet and ask for a third sit. As you go through this exercise, your dog's focus goes from you and getting your attention and over to what you want him to do next. You get him into training mode.

DEPENDING on your dog's level of excitement, you might do anywhere from three to five sits each time you enter the house. After you do this for a little while, your dog will take the shortcut to his reward. Then when you enter the house, your dog will sit in spot number one before you have a chance to ask him to. As soon as he gulps that treat, he will race you to spot number two without being asked and then on to the final sit spot. At this point, you can start to phase out the sits. You will eventually be left with a new habit when you come home.

Chewing

No one likes it when their dog sinks his teeth into their stuff. The big reasons dogs chew things are boredom, insufficient exercise, and lack of supervision. Since dogs don't have hands, the only way to really get into trouble is with their mouth. And "in trouble" is exactly what dogs will be in these circumstances. Don't give your dog too much freedom too quickly. If he's chewing inappropriate things in your home, his behavior tells you he's not ready for it just yet. You need to supervise him closely and teach him what's okay for him to chew on and what is off-limits.

THE EASY METHOD

Remember that your dog has energy and will come out somehow every day, and your dog didn't read the label that said "dog toy" on that squeaky toy you gave him. To him, the carpeting, couch pillows, or wall molding look just as much like a good dog toy. Keep his world small, and when you can't supervise, confine him until he's built good habits of not ripping into your stuff.

I ALSO LIKE to rotate toys and bones regularly to keep things interesting. Have a few of your dog's favorite toys, chew bones, and others tucked away. Switch them out every week or so to keep the toys fresh and exciting. You may also want to keep a few special bones or chew toys for those occasions when you can't supervise as much or need some time to do your own thing.

The Role of Exercise

Exercise is a basic canine need that must be met each and every day. Most destructive behaviors that plague dog owners directly result from a lack of exercise. Exercise is the simplest and the most overlooked tool to greatly reduce problem behaviors in the home. It's always part of my treatment for any behavior issue because everything is positively affected by the release of pent-up energy.

MOST PEOPLE greatly underestimate the amount of exercise that their dog needs. Remember, a tired dog is a good dog—always! There's a good chance you're not providing the exercise your dog requires, so he will find a destructive outlet for that energy. It's your job to ensure you're taking care of your dogs' needs (some breeds and older dogs have more needs than others, too). Find creative, constructive ways to provide your dog with the exercise he so desperately needs, and you'll see many problem behaviors just disappear.

Barking

A dog that barks is the most annoying thing in the world. Dogs bark for several reasons, and some dogs are just louder than others. If you have a dog, you must put up with some barking at reasonable times. After all, they're dogs, and it's one of the things they do. But there's a big difference between some appropriate barking and incessant, nonstop yapping. The treatment depends on the situation. Let's look at some of the most common reasons dogs bark.

BARKING at you

MOST OF THE TIME, your dog barks at you for attention, and you may somehow reward it. Ignoring the barking in this situation, as with jumping, is the best way to get rid of it. Although acknowledging the dog (including disciplining the dog) may be viewed as a reward (negative attention is still attention), withholding attention is the worst discipline you can bestow on your dog. However, ignoring your dog is much easier said than done. If you can put up with his barking long enough for him to realize it's not working, he'll eventually stop. You can give him attention, playtime, a treat, or whatever else he requests when the barking finally stops.

BARKING at the Window

. . .

WATCH any dog cartoon and you'll learn that all dogs do two things: chase cats and bark at the mail carrier. The cat-chasing we can chalk up to a run-of-the-mill species rivalry, but why the mail carrier? After all, the mail carrier seems pretty nice—the only crime they're guilty of committing is delivering too many bills. So why do so many dogs go into a frenzy when they approach your house daily?

THE ANSWER IS simple when you understand your dog's perspective. The mail carrier approaches, and your dog thinks, "Look at this stranger coming up to my house. I'm going to bark at the top of my lungs to scare them away." The mail carrier then drops mail in the box and walks away. Your dog thinks, "That's right. You'd better get out of here. Ha! I managed to scare the thug away. Yeah, I did it! "

YOUR DOG IS REWARDED every time the mail carrier leaves because he believes his reaction is what sent them on their way. The same is true for passing people and dogs. They approach your home, your dog reacts, and they leave. Fido believes he is doing an excellent job of guarding the perimeter. This is why it is impossible to treat your dog's barking at people and other dogs as they pass by your house. To successfully work on this issue, you would need to control the person coming toward the house. They would have to stop when your dog reacts and wait while you work with him to get him back to a calm state of mind. Only then could they continue on their way. Just try getting your mail carrier to do that.

. . .

So, when you can't effectively treat the issue, you need to manage it. If at all possible, limit your dog's access to the front window, at least during high-traffic times. I know it sounds like a training evasion, but there is no other way to address this behavior. Dogs that react to people and other dogs passing by are more likely to carry this habit outside and react while on a leash.

Sometimes you have to accept that the situation is uncontrollable and focus on finding ways to manage it rather than solving it. Pull the shades or keep your dog away from lookout points if you can. Otherwise, his barking will likely get worse with each repetition, and your mail carrier may start throwing those Ikea catalogs at your front window.

Barking on walks

Reactivity on a leash is probably the most common behavioral issue people call me about. It's also the hardest to address because, much like barking out the window, it requires you to control the environment and the other people and dogs involved. Dogs bark at people and other dogs on leash for several reasons: lack of socialization, anxiety, or excitement. Since you can't usually control the people and dogs you'll encounter in public, it's best to just focus on the one thing you do have influence over—your dog.

The best way to stop your dog from being distracted by anything in the outdoor environment is to get his attention off the distractions and onto you. Take some yummy treats along on your walks, and when your dog is walking nicely without any distractions around, make some sound. I use a kissy sound, but you can choose whatever you like—you can even call his name. Give your dog a treat as soon as he looks up at you. Keep repeating this until your dog immediately looks at you whenever you make the sound or say his name.

ONCE YOUR DOG responds well on a walk without distractions, start asking for his attention around mild distractions, like when a dog or person is very far away. Keep working on it, gradually increasing the proximity to the distractions until you're able to get your dog's eye contact, removing his focus on everything around him and keeping it on you. This is more management than treatment, but the less you can control a situation, the more you have to move toward management as a solution.

Digging

Digging up your garden, tunneling under the back fence to the dog next door, or just seeing if he can make it to Earth's core by digging straight down the center of your backyard seems like great fun for your dog, but it probably doesn't go over well with you. Most people see a fenced-in yard as a big plus for dogs, but I see it as a huge negative. To me, a fenced-in yard means the dog is less likely to be walked on the street and will probably be left unattended in the backyard for long periods, usually with nothing to do. If that's the case, it's no surprise that your dog will actively search the area for anything remotely interesting to pass the time.

THE EASY METHOD

. . .

LEAVING your dog alone is asking him to make up his own fun, and he'll do that—as dogs do—so don't be surprised if he comes back in covered in mud, leaving you with a yard that looks like a large block of Swiss cheese. You need to take the time to show your dog what is and is not appropriate in your yard. Some breeds are more likely to dig because it's wired into their DNA. Breeds like dachshunds and terriers were bred to chase small animals down holes and were encouraged to dig after them. As with all breeding, people got what they wanted, so you shouldn't be surprised when it happens. You'll need to watch digging breeds even more closely in the backyard because they will feel compelled to see what they can unearth.

IF DIGGING IS something your dog loves and can't seem to stop doing, you can pick one spot in the yard where it's okay for him to have his fun. Pick a corner, put in some loose dirt or sand, and bury cool stuff for your dog to dig up, like toys and bones. If you encourage your dog to dig to his heart's content in this area, he will learn that's where all the good stuff is hidden and leave the rest of your yard alone.

YOU CAN ALSO HIDE stuff around the yard before you let your dog out there and then play "find it," encouraging him to sniff out and find his surprises. I like to use frozen Kongs for this because after my dog tracks it down, he then has to spend 15 to 20 minutes working at it, which will tire him out more and occupy more of his time.

Jumping On the Counter/Tables

Different dog sizes present unique challenges and issues. If you have a small dog, he's probably under your feet and getting into things under the bed. If you have a larger dog, you have an entirely different set of issues, which usually include him inspecting what's on your countertops and kitchen table. Does your dog put his two big front paws up on the counter to see if anything yummy is up there (also amusingly known as counter surfing), or even better, jump right on top of the counter or table to take a look, a sniff, and a lick?

EVEN THOUGH THIS usually affects the big guys, those little furry creatures can also get there if given the right motivation and something to climb on. Almost every dog owner has a story about leaving their lunch on the table for a second or thawing something for dinner on the counter and returning to only crumbs or paw prints. Can you really blame your dog, though? It's so tempting and smells so good that it's hard to leave it alone. No, you can't really blame him, but you can train him. You can teach your dog to leave your countertops alone and respect your wishes to be the one eating those delectable treats if you put in the time and effort.

Puppy-Proofing

The best precaution is never to leave your dog alone when snacks are out on the counter. Although it seems like a straightforward question, many people just assume their dog will be fine. Not me. Assume that he'll try to eat anything that smells good to him. He's a dog, and dogs enjoy eating foods that smell good. If you cannot supervise your dog, you must either remove the temptations or keep him away from the kitchen. That's a great way to manage the situation, but if you want to be able to leave stuff on your table without the worry that your lunch will be gone if you turn your back for a second, you'll need to work with your dog and show him how to properly behave.

Resource Control

You must teach your dog what is and is not acceptable in the kitchen and correct any counter-surf attempts. Remember that the earlier you catch a dog on the wrong path, the easier it is to turn him around and the less effort it takes to get him to withdraw. You can remove your dog's paws from the counter, but you've taught him nothing and he's done yet another negative repetition. You need to supervise him, maybe even entice him with something tasty on the counter, and wait for that first glimmer in his eye. Then give a quick verbal correction (I use a sharp "Hey!" or "Eh-eh!"). If you successfully catch him at the beginning of his thought and action process, that usually works fine. If not, move in between him and the counter (the resource) and back him up a little.

YOU'RE ESSENTIALLY a goalie defending the counter from your dog, but you must be a calm goalie, moving slowly and confidently. You're simply telling your dog that he can't use the kitchen counter right now. You may have to do this several times. You want to step aside, so your dog has an open path to the counter but doesn't use it. To make this work, you need to catch him as early as possible in his thought process.

Separation Anxiety

Having a close bond with our canine companions is one of the greatest parts of dog ownership for humans and dogs. But what if your dog is so attached to you that he panics whenever he can't be with you?

IF YOUR DOG barks or howls constantly while you're gone, destroys your walls or furniture, or has potty accidents that only happen when he's home alone, he may have separation anxiety.

AS THE NAME IMPLIES, this is a behavioral disorder that causes your dog to become incredibly stressed and upset whenever he's left alone. Separation anxiety can be a challenging problem to deal with, especially in severe cases. Some dogs cause thousands of dollars worth of damage to their owners' homes, make so much noise that neighbors complain, or even injure themselves trying to escape a crate or room in which they're confined.

WITH PATIENCE AND CONSISTENCY, most dog owners can significantly improve their pet's anxiety level, making life easier for everyone.

Helping Your Dog Cope with Separation Anxiety

Get Him Nice and Tired

. . .

GIVE YOUR DOG MORE EXERCISE, especially just before you leave the house each day. While this won't solve an anxiety problem on its own, dogs who aren't getting sufficient exercise will often have more pent-up, nervous energy. This can contribute to panting, pacing, and crying when you leave.

TO DO A BETTER job of this, adjust your schedule a bit if needed. Take your dog for a long walk in the morning before work or play a quick game of fetch in the backyard. If he's pleasantly tired from running and playing, he'll likely lie down for a nap once you're gone.

Give Your Dog More Space

Try allowing your pup more room to move around if you can do this safely. For many dogs with separation anxiety, being confined in a crate or small room can increase their panic and worsen the problem.

TRY LEAVING your dog loose in a larger part of the house while you're gone. In some cases, this can make a big difference in your dog's comfort level and dramatically improve his behavior.

Skip the Drama

Keep your arrivals and departures quiet and low-key. I know this is tough for most of us. But giving long, dramatic goodbyes when you leave and celebrating with lots of excitement when you come home can make things worse. It only reinforces the idea that all the fun happens when you're there and makes the house seem extra quiet and lonely after you leave.

INSTEAD, be calm and matter-of-fact about entering and leaving the house. You can casually greet your dog when you get home but go about your normal routine without paying much attention to him until he settles down.

Leave Him with Something Special

Give your dog an extra-tasty, long-lasting treat each time you leave. Try puzzle toys such as a Twist 'n Treat stuffed with spray cheese or a Kong packed full of kibble and peanut butter. Bully sticks or pig ears can also be good options for some dogs. This gives your pup something positive to look forward to and helps keep him busy while he's home alone.

Monitor From Afar

Use video recording technology to monitor your dog while you're gone. Video recording your dog while you're gone can be incredibly helpful since this allows you to see changes in his anxiety level daily. You can then modify your strategy based on what you see. Try using in-home surveillance equipment if you have some already, or use your tablet or webcam. You can also use a video camcorder on a tripod.

Consider Medication

Talk to your veterinarian about your pup's anxiety issues. This is crucial if your dog is causing significant damage to your home or injuring himself. For severe cases of separation anxiety, it can be very difficult to make progress at first without some prescription medication on board. Your vet will help you decide if this would be a good option for your pup and will prescribe an appropriate drug to help control his anxiety if needed.

Teaching an Alternate Behavior

In addition to the technique just described, you can demonstrate the behavior you would like your dog to exhibit. This works really well if it happens routinely, like when you're making dinner. You know what you don't want your dog to do, so before he goes down that predictable path, teach him what you would prefer and make it really rewarding for him, so he's happy to do it.

YOU WILL TEACH your dog to just sit and watch while you're in the kitchen making dinner, eating lunch, or in any other situation where he might try to jump up on the counters. First, start practicing this when there's no food on the counter and you're not busy making a meal. Once you've shaped his new behavior with some repetitions, you can work on it with some food and, finally, while you're actually cooking.

PUT your bait food item on the counter and move your dog where you want him to be either by backing him into it by moving your body into his space or by luring him with a treat. If you've practiced your wait command, this is a great time to use it. Once he's in the right spot, slowly back away. If your dog moves forward, mark it with some sort of verbal cue ("Hey!" or "Eh-eh!") to let him know he made a mistake and move into his space to back him into the spot again. You aim to have your dog stay put while you grab something off the kitchen counter. Please wait for a moment, then bring one of his treats and reward him. Repeat this, frequently rewarding at first (maybe every couple of seconds) and then slowly increasing the time between rewards. Your dog can enjoy free delivery if he remains at his designated spot.

It's VERY important to practice this before you start working with higher-value food. Think of Thanksgiving dinner and all those smells. Soon, whenever you go into the kitchen to cook, your dog will automatically go to his spot because that's the most rewarding place in the house—the place where he gets free delivery for just sitting there. For a dog, it doesn't get any better than that.

When to Seek Professional Help

You can address most of these common problems by yourself with some time and effort. However, suppose you've been working hard at an issue and just can't seem to get past it. In that case, the behavior is getting worse over time, or you're just not sure how to address it, it might be time to call in a professional dog trainer to take a look at your situation and walk you through the treatment. If you're not sure what you're doing or have lots of questions, hiring a good trainer to guide you is a wise investment. Bringing in a trainer will greatly shorten your learning curve and get you on the right track so you can enjoy your dog more. The sooner you recognize that you need help—and get it—the better. If you wait and let your dog repeat a behavior, it will take longer to address, and the process will be more difficult.

. . .

THERE ARE many different kinds of dog trainers out there, each with their own training philosophies and techniques. Make sure you research to find one who best suits your ideals and does training that you're comfortable with. Look for someone who uses positive and reward-based training is well respected in the field, and has several good reviews online. You should hire someone you get along with, who is good with both people and dogs.

11

GOOD CARE WILL HELP KEEP YOUR DOG HEALTHY

Most dog owners probably don't think much about basic pet care tasks like bathing, brushing, or nail trimming, until the time comes to do them and your dog doesn't want to cooperate. Many dogs are nervous, fearful, or even aggressive about simple handling and grooming because they've never been taught what you want them to do.

IT MIGHT SURPRISE you that your dog can easily be trained to cooperate with you when you need to do these things, just like learning to sit or lie down on command. You'll find this easiest if you have a young puppy who's new to the entire process, but even adult dogs with a history of being anxious about handling can learn to relax. This makes things much less stressful for both of you and much safer.

IN THIS SECTION, you'll find easy step-by-step guidelines for teaching your dog to allow every kind of basic care or grooming task you're likely to encounter—everything from routine dental care to bathing and brushing, nail trimming, and even taking medication. The specific steps are different depending on the task you're working on (teeth brushing, giving a bath, and so forth), but the basic approach is the same in every case: go slowly, be patient, and stay positive.

WITH A LITTLE PRACTICE, you (or your vet or groomer) should be able to provide any care your dog needs to keep him clean and healthy!

Standing Still for a Physical Exam

Teaching your dog to stand still for an exam might not seem very flashy or exciting, but you'd be surprised how much easier it makes things at the vet's office. For many dogs, having their body handled can be uncomfortable or scary if they haven't been taught what to expect, making it hard to get a thorough checkup.

YOU CAN ALSO USE this skill at home to check your dog regularly for lumps or bumps, skin problems, or other issues that you might not notice otherwise.

TO TRAIN your dog to stand still for a physical exam:

START With Your Dog Standing

. . .

STANDING IS the best position for an exam because it allows you (or your veterinarian) to carefully palpate your dog's belly and chest, check the rear legs and tail, and even examine your pup's "private areas" if needed. These things are very hard to do if your dog sits on his rear end or is wiggling around. Problems can easily be missed without a nice solid stand.

TRY a Light Touch

TOUCH YOUR DOG gently on the back with one hand. Praise and reward if he stands still while you do this. If not, just remind him to stand and try again.

STROKE HIS BACK and Sides

REPEAT STEP 2 several times until your dog confidently holds his position each time you touch his back. Run your hand gently down his back and sides as if you were petting him, with praise and treats for standing still.

WORK UP To Doing More

TRY TOUCHING his front and rear legs, chest, and belly. Continue to praise and reward after running your hand over each new area.

. . .

HANDLE SENSITIVE AREAS Gently

FINALLY, move on to more sensitive parts of his body, such as the paws, tail, ears, and genital areas. If he gets nervous and pulls away, just go back to something easier for the next few repetitions and work your way up again. Remember, this can be challenging for many dogs, so go slowly and be patient.

COMPLETE a Full Exam

EVENTUALLY, you can work your way up to doing a full examination while your dog stands calmly for a single treat at the end. Practice at home at least once a month to ensure your dog remembers what to do. Your veterinarian will thank you for this, and you'll be satisfied knowing he's getting a thorough checkup at each visit.

Nail Trimming

From our perspective, it can be hard to understand why nail trimming is so difficult for many dogs. After all, if done properly, there's no pain and very little drama. But from your dog's point of view, handling his feet may be scary and uncomfortable.

MANY DOGS HAVE SENSITIVE PAWS; your dog may not understand why you're trying to touch them. Furthermore, if your dog has had a bad experience with nail trimming, he will likely remember it and may be afraid of having his toes cut.

· · ·

FORTUNATELY, any dog can learn to relax and be comfortable while you gently trim his nails. It just takes some patience and a good training plan.

TO TEACH your dog to stand calmly for nail trims:

GET everything ready

YOU MAY FIND it easiest for large dogs to sit on the floor with him. If your dog is smaller, you could opt to use a grooming table instead. Make sure you have a supply of tasty treats and your nail clippers handy.

IF YOUR DOG seems nervous as soon as he sees the nail trimmers, spend the first several training sessions allowing your dog to sniff the clippers without doing anything else. Please make this a positive experience with lots of praise and treats, and don't move on to the next step until he seems relaxed and comfortable.

TRY TOUCHING the Paws

START by gently touching one of your dog's paws at your fingertips, then praise and reward. Do this with each paw separately to ensure he's comfortable with all four feet touching before moving on.

. . .

IF HE RESISTS or tries to pull away, don't scold him; this will only make him more anxious. Instead, simply back up a step or two and take it easy. Reward when he is calm again.

INTRODUCE the Clippers

GENTLY LIFT one paw and touch it lightly with the nail clippers. Praise and reward him for standing still. Repeat this with each paw in turn. Work your way up to touching each toenail gently, one at a time.

CLIP THE TIP of One Toenail

DON'T CUT the nail too short because you might cut into the quick. Cut the tip of one toenail, then praise and reward once this is done.

IT'S BEST NOT to try and trim all of his nails in the same session at first. Instead, do one or two nails and then stop. You want to end the session on a high note.

DO A FULL NAIL Trim

WORK UP to this step slowly to ensure your dog is comfortable with the process. The first several times you try a complete nail trim, reward with a treat after clipping each nail. All the while, make sure your dog is relaxed and happy.

. . .

THE NUMBER of sessions required to complete all five steps of nail trimming will vary from dog to dog. Puppies who are "starting fresh" with no previous history of scary nail trims will likely progress very quickly, while older dogs who have had negative experiences in the past may take considerably longer.

TAKE AS LONG as your dog needs, and don't rush the process. Being able to do easy, stress-free nail trims for the rest of his life is well worth it.

Ear Cleaning

Regular ear cleaning is crucial for maintaining your dog's health, especially if he has large "drop ears" like a Labrador retriever or cocker spaniel. Done correctly, this should not be a painful procedure for your dog, but it can feel strange to him and may be scary if he isn't accustomed to it. To clean your dog's ears, you can use an over-the-counter ear flush labeled for dogs or ask your veterinarian for a recommendation.

TO TEACH your dog to stand quietly for ear cleaning:

GET Your Supplies Ready

START by gathering everything you need: ear cleaner, cotton balls or a soft washcloth, and lots of treats.

. . .

LET Your Dog Get Comfortable

SIT on the floor with your dog or sit on a couch or chair if you prefer. Allow him to sniff everything if he's curious.

IF HE ALREADY HAS A HISTORY OF being nervous about ear cleaning, you may need to spend several sessions on this particular step. Praise and reward him for staying near you and looking at everything, and don't go any further until he's calm and relaxed.

TOUCH THE EARS

GENTLY TOUCH ONE EAR, then praise and reward. Repeat with the other ear. Do this severally until your dog is completely comfortable with this step.

INTRODUCE the Bottle

PICK up the bottle of ear cleaner (still securely closed), and bring it up to your dog's ear as if to squirt some into the ear canal. You don't want to actually use the cleaner yet, so don't open the nozzle. Touch the bottle of cleaner to your dog's ear, then praise and reward.

. . .

Y<small>OUR DOG MAY BE</small> nervous about this step at first, especially if he has not enjoyed having his ears cleaned in the past. That's okay. Just take your time and go slowly. Repeat this as many times as needed, giving a treat each time until he's calm and relaxed.

A<small>DD</small> *the Cleaner*

O<small>PEN</small> the bottle of ear cleaner. Gently squirt the recommended number of drops into your dog's ear canal. Praise enthusiastically and reward. This is a strange sensation for most dogs, so your pup may appear startled. If he appears anxious, compliment him on his good behavior and give him lots of treats.

R<small>ED</small>, swollen ears, excessive discharge, and an unpleasant odor coming from the ear are all symptoms of an ear infection in your dog. In that case, see your veterinarian before attempting to clean the ears at home.

A<small>N INFECTED EAR</small> will be very sore and painful, so don't try to work through the cleaning steps until the infection is resolved.

C<small>LEAN</small> *the Ears*

W<small>ORK UP</small> to being able to clean ears. Fill the ear canal with a cleaning solution, massage the ear, and then use your cotton balls or washcloth to wipe away any gunk or discharge. Remove your hands and let your dog shake his head. This is the final step, so give your pup lots of praise and a great reward when you get there! Repeat the process with the other ear.

Dental Care

I know—brushing your dog's teeth can seem daunting at first, especially if you've never done it. But the truth is, good dental care is just as important for your dog's overall health as yours.

TARTAR BUILDUP CAN LEAD to painful dental problems such as gingivitis, tooth root infections, and tooth loss. It can even damage internal organs like the heart and kidneys by seeding your dog's bloodstream with bacteria. So starting a good dental care plan early on is well worth it.

TO TEACH your dog to be comfortable having his teeth brushed:

GET Your Supplies

START by selecting a comfortable toothbrush and an appropriate dog-friendly toothpaste. You can either order online or purchase at most pet stores. Your veterinarian's office may carry them for sale too. Canine toothbrushes should be very soft, so they don't cause pain or irritation to the gums.

. . .

ENSURE to use toothpaste that is specifically designed for dogs. Human toothpaste has too much fluoride and is not safe to use. Most dog toothpastes come in canine-friendly flavors like chicken or beef, so you shouldn't have trouble finding one your dog likes.

FIND a Comfortable Spot to Work

DEPENDING on what's easiest for you, you can sit on the floor or put your dog on a grooming table. You could even hold him in your lap if you prefer if he's a small breed.

LET Your Dog Try The Toothpaste

LET your dog lick a small amount of toothpaste off your finger. He'll most likely think this is a fantastic treat. Repeat this several times until your dog's tail happily wags at the sight of the toothpaste tube.

RUB Your Finger Across His Teeth

MOST DOGS ENJOY THIS STEP, as long as they like the toothpaste you're using. Praise your dog and tell him what a good boy he is while you gently touch all of his teeth, from the tiny incisors in the front to the larger molars in the back.

. . .

IF YOUR DOG is comfortable and relaxed, you can gently open his mouth to reach the inside surfaces of the teeth. This makes some dogs a bit more nervous, so work up to this gradually.

INTRODUCE the Toothbrush

YOU CAN LET your dog lick some of the toothpaste off the brush.

IF YOUR DOG has severe dental disease already (red or swollen gums, exposed tooth roots, pus, or a foul odor coming from his mouth), please see your veterinarian before starting a tooth brushing regimen at home.

BRUSHING your pup's teeth is great for preventing problems down the line and keeping his mouth healthy, but it won't fix existing dental issues. Your veterinarian can perform a complete dental cleaning under anesthesia and will remove any painful or infected teeth so you'll have a clean slate to start with.

GENTLY USE the Brush To Touch His Teeth

REPEAT STEP 4, using the toothbrush instead of your finger. This will be a different sensation for your dog, so he might be nervous at first. If he pulls away or seems uncomfortable, stop and go more slowly. You may need to do just one or two teeth at a time until he gets more accustomed to the brush.

BRUSH the Teeth Regularly To Keep Them Clean

EVENTUALLY, you can work up to being able to brush all of your dog's teeth easily in one sitting. For best results, make this part of his daily routine, just before bedtime or first thing in the morning immediately he gets up.

Bathing Your Dog

For many dogs and owners, bathing can be a stressful experience that provokes anxiety on both sides. Most dogs don't enjoy getting wet or being restrained in a scary tub with water running, and no owner enjoys wrestling with a frantic pup who's covered in shampoo and desperate to escape the bathroom.

EVEN IF YOUR dog isn't a fan of soap and water, there's no reason he can't learn to relax happily in the bathtub when he needs a good wash.

TO TEACH your dog to stand calmly for a bath:

GET Your Dog Comfortable In the Bathroom

· · ·

START by bringing your dog into the bathroom and closing the door. If your pup has a history of scary bath experiences, he may become very anxious at this point, and that's okay. Spend several short training sessions sitting in the bathroom, praising and feeding him treats. Don't progress until he's happy and relaxed, even with the door closed.

REWARD FOR GETTING *In the Tub*

TAKE some peanut butter or spray cheese and smear a generous amount inside the bathtub. If your dog is fairly small, pick him up and put him in the tub; if he's larger, show him the yummy treat waiting and encourage him to hop in. Let him stand in the tub, lick the goodies for a few minutes, and then lift him out again.

REMEMBER—NO water in the tub just yet. Right now, you should focus on getting your dog happy and comfortable in the bathtub. Please don't add water until he's happily jumping into the tub on his own, or wagging his tail eagerly for you to lift him in.

INTRODUCE *the Water*

WHEN YOUR DOG is happy to hop in the tub and stand there while licking his treat, slowly turn on the water. Ensure the temperature is just right and the stream is moving slowly enough that he won't be startled by the noise. Complement him on being such a good boy. Run 2 or 3 inches of water into the tub, then stop. Check to see if your dog is showing any signs of stress and is still licking his peanut butter. If he is, repeat this process until he is unfazed by the water.

Wet the Coat, Shampoo, and Rinse

If your dog is comfortable and relaxed standing in a few inches of water, bathe him. You can pour water over him using a pitcher or wet him down using a handheld sprayer attachment if you have one. Add shampoo, lather, and rinse thoroughly. Just go slowly, and make sure to replenish his supply of peanut butter as often as needed to keep him busy.

Fade Out the Treats

Over time, you can decrease the amount of peanut butter you use for each bath. If your dog seems comfortable, you can eventually phase it out altogether. Just praise him for standing still in the tub and watch him closely for any signs of stress. Many dogs learn to enjoy their "spa time" after a while, as long as you're patient and gentle.

Brushing Your Dog

If your dog has a short, smooth hair coat like a miniature pinscher or Weimaraner—lucky you! You're free to skip this section.

. . .

FOR THE REST OF US, **brushing our dogs is a daily reality.** This can be a real challenge if your dog gets nervous or won't stand still when the brush comes out. Unfortunately, basic grooming isn't optional if you want to maintain healthy skin and hair.

GOOD GROOMING HABITS are easy to start with a new puppy, but even adult dogs who may not care much for brushing can learn to relax and stand quietly so that you can groom without a fuss.

TO TEACH your dog to stand still for brushing:

FIND a Comfortable Spot to Work

IF YOUR PUP is small to medium-sized, you'll probably find it best to use a grooming table—it's much easier on your back than leaning over your dog to reach everything. Working on the floor is usually the simplest option for large or giant breeds.

GATHER YOUR GROOMING Tools

AT A MINIMUM, you'll need a good-quality pin brush, wire slicker brush, a spray bottle of water, or a leave-in conditioner. Depending on your dog's coat type, you may also need a wide-toothed comb, soft bristle brush, or an undercoat rake.

. . .

GET *Your Dog Comfortable*

PUT him on the grooming table or bring him to the area where you plan to work. Let him see and sniff the brushes and other grooming tools if he wants. Many dogs are curious about these objects at first. Make sure he's calm and relaxed before moving on to the next step.

ASK *Your Dog to Stand*

IF HE DOESN'T KNOW this cue yet, see Steps to Training "Stand" in Part I for instructions on how to teach it.

INTRODUCE *the Brush*

LIGHTLY STROKE your dog's back once with the brush. If he stands still, praise him and reward him with a treat. Ask him to stand and try again if he wiggles or pulls away. Please repeat this step until he can stand solidly without moving while you lightly brush his back.

SPRAY *Lightly With Water*

WHEN HE'S comfortable being touched by the brush, add a spritz of water or conditioner; this keeps the fur damp while you're brushing, which is important to avoid damaging the coat. Praise and reward him for standing still. Then repeat a single brushstroke down his back, as in step 5.

Work Up To the Rest of His Body

YOU CAN GRADUALLY PROGRESS to brushing his legs, sides, chest, and tail as long as he's doing well. Praise and reward for every few brushstrokes first, then work up to brushing for longer and longer periods without a treat. If he moves, just remind him to stand and wait until he's comfortable before continuing.

ALTERNATIVELY, while you brush, you can have a helper stand nearby and feed treats periodically or hold a spoonful of peanut butter or spray cheese for your dog to lick.

Give Your Dog a Complete Brushing

EVENTUALLY, your dog should be able to stand still for an entire brushing session (up to twenty to thirty minutes) for a single treat at the end. Just go slowly and don't rush the process. This is an important life skill for your dog to learn, so it pays to take the time to teach it correctly!

Administering Medication

Even if your dog is currently healthy, chances are he will require medication at some point in his life: antibiotics for an infection, nonsteroidal anti-inflammatory drugs (NSAIDs) for arthritis, and so forth. Convincing him to swallow a pill can be challenging if you've never had to deal with this before.

FORTUNATELY, medicating your dog doesn't need to be a struggle. With a little planning and foresight, you can do many things to make this much easier for both of you.

TO TEACH your dog to take medication easily:

COMBINE It with Food

TRY MIXING the meds into a tasty treat, if possible. Liquid medications can usually be mixed with a spoonful of something stinky and delicious, such as canned cat food or liverwurst—this is a very effective way of disguising the taste and convincing your dog to take his medicine voluntarily. Tablets can often be crushed and mixed into soft food like this as well.

ALWAYS CHECK with your veterinarian to ensure this is okay, especially when a new medicine is prescribed for your pup. In most cases, it's fine to mix your dog's medication with food. However, there may be some situations when the drug needs to be given on an empty stomach. Other restrictions might limit what you can mix it with. When in doubt, ask.

. . .

HIDE It in A Treat

FOR PILLS or capsules that can't be crushed, put them inside a soft, smelly treat: a piece of cheese, a slice of hot dog, or commercial Pill Pockets are all good options. If your dog takes the treat gingerly and spits out the medication, try giving several treats in a row. Hide the "medicated" treat with the others and give them quickly, one after the other, so that he doesn't have time to think too much about chewing.

TRAIN Your Dog to Take The Meds

IF YOUR DOG doesn't take medication hidden in food, you can teach him to allow you to administer the meds on their own. This doesn't need to be stressful or unpleasant; just teach him what to expect and make sure to reward him afterward for cooperating.

FOR PILLS, START BY "PILLING" your dog with treats to help him get used to the procedure. Get him to open his mouth, put a piece of meat or cheese on the back of his tongue, and push it down with your finger. Ask your vet to show you how if you're nervous about your technique. After your dog has accepted the "pill" treats, you can transition to the real thing. Praise and reward with a yummy treat after he's done.

FOR LIQUID MEDICATIONS, ask your veterinarian for an oral syringe with which you can practice. Draw up a small amount of something tasty, such as chicken or beef broth, and use the syringe to give it to your dog. Gently place the tip of the syringe in the back corner of his mouth, then depress the plunger to squirt in the liquid. Go slowly so that he has time to swallow without getting choked. Once he's comfortable with this, use the same technique to give liquid medication when needed. Again, praise and reward with a treat immediately afterward.

CONCLUSION

People adore their furry friends. However, not every moment is pleasurable if your dog has not been trained to perform specific behaviors or avoid undesirable behaviors. At first glance, dog training may appear somewhat overwhelming, particularly if you are a first-time dog owner. The reality is that training your dog is a massive undertaking. If you approach the task incrementally, you will find it much less frightening. This book gives straightforward yet useful information in a step-by-step approach to assist new dog owners in learning how to train their dogs.

If you found my experiences and guidance has benefitted you and your dog, I would ask that you share what you have learned from this book or leave a favorable review on Amazon. I hope you will enjoy every minute as you learn and grow with your new best friend.

Best of luck!